D1623844

At ✳ Issue

Are Privacy Rights Being Violated?

Stuart A. Kallen, *Book Editor*

Bruce Glassman, *Vice President*
Bonnie Szumski, *Publisher*
Helen Cothran, *Managing Editor*

GREENHAVEN PRESS
An imprint of Thomson Gale, a part of The Thomson Corporation

THOMSON
━━━━✳━━━━ ™
GALE

Detroit • New York • San Francisco • San Diego • New Haven, Conn.
Waterville, Maine • London • Munich

© 2006 Thomson Gale, a part of The Thomson Corporation.

Thomson and Star Logo are trademarks and Gale and Greenhaven Press are registered trademarks used herein under license.

For more information, contact
Greenhaven Press
27500 Drake Rd.
Farmington Hills, MI 48331-3535
Or you can visit our Internet site at http://www.gale.com

ALL RIGHTS RESERVED.
No part of this work covered by the copyright hereon may be reproduced or used in any form or by any means—graphic, electronic, or mechanical, including photocopying, recording, taping, Web distribution or information storage retrieval systems—without the written permission of the publisher.

Every effort has been made to trace the owners of copyrighted material.

Cover credit: © Planet Art

LIBRARY OF CONGRESS CATALOGING-IN-PUBLICATION DATA
Are privacy rights being violated? / Stuart A. Kallen, book editor.
p. cm. — (At issue)
Includes bibliographical references and index.
ISBN 0-7377-2360-2 (lib. : alk. paper) — ISBN 0-7377-2361-0 (pbk. : alk. paper)
1. Privacy, Right of—United States. I. Kallen, Stuart A., 1955– . II. At issue (San Diego, Calif.)
KF1262.A97 2006
342.7308'58—dc22   2005045117

Printed in the United States of America

Contents

Introduction

English author George Orwell wrote his novel *1984* in the years following World War II. The book envisions a society dominated by a totalitarian government, known as "Big Brother," that monitors peoples' every move through television-like screens in homes, offices, and businesses. Citizens have no privacy and expect none as ubiquitous posters remind them that "Big Brother is watching you."

When Orwell published his novel in 1949, technology was much less advanced than it is today. There were no surveillance cameras on street corners or supercomputers analyzing billions of credit card transactions. More than fifty-five years later, however, some privacy rights advocates argue that the world depicted in *1984* has come to pass. As author Richard A. Glenn explains in *The Right to Privacy: Rights and Liberties Under the Law:*

> Closed-circuit TVs scrutinize activities in supermarkets, shopping malls, workplaces, and along city streets. Traffic monitoring systems record the whereabouts of automobiles. Wireless communications technology can pinpoint the location of cellular phones. Electronic communications systems generate information about an individual's credit-card purchases and Internet browsing habits. Computer technology provides the means for central storage of and easy accessibility to massive amounts of data, making information collection much easier. And the Internet . . . facilitates the unprecedented and rapid dissemination of stored information.

The development of technologies such as those described above has led to many limitations on privacy in the United States. Police can use video cameras to monitor people walking down a city street—or record the actions of people protesting at a demonstration. Banks, convenience stores, and other businesses have the right to use video surveillance cameras to record the comings and goings of customers. Businesses can also collect credit information, records of purchases, Social Security numbers, and other financial data about customers. Furthermore, there are few restrictions on the rights of businesses to monitor their employees in the workplace. A 2000 study of human resources professionals at more than seven hundred companies revealed that 74 percent of employers monitor workers' Internet use at work; 72 percent check their employees' e-mails; and 51 percent review employees' phone calls.

Even as modern technologies encroach on personal privacy in dozens of ways, many Americans still value their right to be left alone. According to an August 2002 survey by the First Amendment Center, 81 percent of those polled reported that the right to privacy was "essential." People are particularly concerned about protecting their privacy because of the rise of identity theft, in which a criminal steals personal identification information—such as an individual's Social Security number or credit card account codes—in order to commit a crime such as obtaining a loan or mortgage or even filing a bankruptcy claim in that person's name. CBSNews.com reported that in 2005 alone, more than five hundred thousand Americans would become the victims of identity theft and that more than $4 billion would be stolen in their names. According to experts it can take anywhere from six months to two years for victims to sort out the financial havoc created by identity thieves.

Given the risks of identity theft, some Americans are wary of even legitimate businesses violating their privacy rights. For example, in a 2002 report to Congress the Federal Trade Commission (FTC) cited a poll showing that 92 percent of respondents from households with Internet access stated that they do not trust online companies to keep their personal information confidential. This lack of trust is estimated by the FTC to cost online retailers as much as $18 billion in lost sales annually.

While many Americans are highly concerned about invasions of privacy, some argue that reports that privacy is dying are highly exaggerated. Amitai Etzioni, the author of *The Limits of Privacy*, writes that although it is not difficult to find U.S. opinion polls that support the argument that Americans fear their privacy rights are in grave danger, these polls ask "cost-free" questions such as whether or not people would like stronger laws to protect their privacy. Etzioni argues that such questions are "like asking if you want more fresh air, good movies, or better government—with no additional effort or expenditure on your part. The only surprise here is that anybody demurs." He states that Americans reveal the true extent of their concern about privacy rights when they are asked to make an effort to protect them. For example, he notes that when people were asked whether they checked the privacy policy of the health and medical Web sites they visited, only one in four claimed they did "despite the fact that medical privacy concerns the most personal information of all." Further, he found that about 80 percent of Americans polled said they were willing to reveal personal information in order to obtain a small discount.

Privacy researcher Alan Westin has also found that the majority of Americans are not deeply worried about the possibility of their privacy rights being violated. He divides the American public into three categories: privacy advocates, who possess very high privacy concerns; privacy pragmatists, who are willing to forgo some privacy for shopping convenience; and the privacy unconcerned, who have little to no concern about privacy issues. According to Westin's research, 125 million Americans make up the privacy pragmatist category, and another 45 million comprises the privacy unconcerned group. The number of people in these two groups combined is nearly three times the 57 million Americans in the privacy advocate group.

Some researchers believe that people who are apparently unconcerned about privacy violations feel this way because they do not understand the extent of the legal rights enjoyed by the government and businesses to gather information about citizens. Communications expert Oscar Gandy has found that the more people read or hear about the potential use and abuse of computerized information, the more worried they become about privacy violations and the less they trust organizations that collect information about consumers.

Although it may be difficult to gauge the extent of people's concern and knowledge about privacy rights, it is certain that as technology continues to develop, new products will be devised that could make Americans more vulnerable to privacy violations. On the other hand, many new devices that protect privacy, such as sophisticated encryption systems for computers, are also being developed. In addition, more laws and regulations are being put in place to protect privacy. It is therefore unclear whether the future will bring greater protection of people's personal information or an erosion of privacy rights. The authors in *At Issue: Are Privacy Rights Being Violated?* explore the current debate over privacy rights and some of the trends that will affect future debate.

1

Companies Use Computer Spyware to Steal Personal Data

Matthew Callan

Matthew Callan writes for the online magazines, or "zines,"
Scratchbomb.com and Freezerbox.com. He is currently work-
ing on his first novel, Breaking My Shoes.

One of the newest tools that advertisers can use to violate a person's privacy rights is known as spyware. This
software is secretly bundled with freeware available on
the Internet. When users download the freeware, they
also unknowingly download spyware that records users'
Web browsing habits and software preferences. The information is transmitted to advertisers who then bom-
bard the victims with an endless array of annoying pop-
up ads. Only the most competent computer users can
detect and delete spyware once it finds its way onto a
hard drive. With few legal limits on this activity, the
privacy of computer users is under attack by unprinci-
pled advertisers who will stop at nothing to steal personal information to make a profit.

Though we have been firmly entrenched in the information
age for almost 20 years now, the Internet still retains a Wild
West atmosphere, without a Wyatt Earp to tame it. Rules are
made and discarded at will, virtue a dead end, pimping a virtue.
You must get yours before the next guy grabs it, any way you
can, and there are plenty of sharpies promising an edge, bottles

Matthew Callan, "Spyware: How Your Personal Data Gets Stolen Online," *Alternet*,
February 8, 2002. Copyright © 2002 by Independent Media Institute. All rights reserved. Reproduced by permission.

of snake oil in hand labeled DRINK ME.

Witness the latest con, spyware, software that is able to swipe personal data from your computer and sell it to the highest bidder. All this is done under the guise of collecting general demographics and providing users with exciting offers, but its potential is far too frightening to ignore.

Spyware usually comes to your computer in the form of a simple data-collection program, bundled along with a piece of freeware (an application that the developer offers to the public gratis) that contains embedded banner ads. As you use the application, the spyware takes the personal information you provided when registering and adds to it other appliction-related data; what you are using the application for, how long you use it, etc. This information is sent to a server that interprets the data in order to target you with very specific advertising.

> **//** *A program you never wanted squats in your computer's hard drive, sending personal information to a company with whom you never had any direct contact and never agreed to give such access.* **//**

Rotating banner ads are like airport surveys: If you want to ignore them, you can. And since most freeware relies on advertising dollars to pay the bills, this may seem a fair price to pay for a programmer's labor (and the reason why these programs are often referred to more benignly as adware). However, there are troubling aspects to this practice; some potential, some already in play.

First of all, users are rarely notified of the presence of any spyware when they download; if so, only in the glaucoma-inducing lines of tiny text that make up a User Agreement. More often than not, spyware is not administered by the company from which users receive the application, but by a third party that markets the spyware. So while you may have agreed to the terms and conditions set forth by the application's developers, you did not specifically agree to anything the spyware's administrator has in store for you. Under current laws, this is all perfectly kosher. Software providers are under no legal obligation to inform the public of their purpose in gathering personal information, let alone how they do it and with whom. Most sites do disclose some information about what software you receive and what it does, merely to give lip service to privacy concerns, knowing full well that their security policies have the same judicial weight as handshake agreements.

Pop-Ups Appear Incessantly

So it was only a matter of time until a program such as VX2 would hit the Web, and hit it hard. VX2 takes spyware to a new level by pulling information, not just from use of an application, but from the use of a computer. When freeware that includes VX2 is installed on a computer, the program saves itself to a directory on the hard drive. Once firmly in place, it keeps track of the user's Web browsing (current and historical), information entered into forms, and configuration of the user's hardware and software. Based on all this information, pop-up ads begin to appear incessantly in the user's Web browser, giving the false impression that the Web page being viewed is responsible for the constant annoyances.

In order to discover that VX2 is on your computer, you would have to determine the IP [identifier number of the computer] of the pop-up ads plaguing your browser, a task that less technically-inclined Web surfers are not able to do. Even harder to determine is how VX2 got on your computer, and where it is stored. To top it all off, VX2 is an incredibly difficult program to completely remove from a hard drive, and doing so often disables the freeware that let it in.

> *Many companies offering freeware attach [spyware] to their software willy-nilly, presumably under the spell of sleazy marketers.*

Even more disturbing information can be culled from the VX2's Privacy Policy, as featured on its Web site. Although VX2 insists that it does not collect any truly damaging data (i.e., credit card information), it does concede that "the operation of certain third party websites may result in some personal information being included in URL data. . . . Such instances are rare and are the result of poor security practices by these third party websites." Thereby, the buck is passed when some mysterious charges suddenly appear on your Visa bill. VX2 also reserves the right to update its software at any time, saying that "upgrades may include third party applications. . . . They will be done automatically in the background while you are surfing the web in order to cause the least amount of inconvenience to our users as possible." Its stated reason for capturing data that the user enters into forms (which includes even secure, encrypted forms) goes past disingenuousness and straight into Orwell country: "This information is automatically sent to VX2 in order to save you the time and trouble of submitting such information to us yourself."

What VX2 boils down to is this: A program you never wanted squats in your computer's hard drive, sending personal information to a company with whom you never had any direct contact and never agreed to give such access; a program that, furthermore, can upgrade itself and add any other program to your computer that it sees fit. It is the kind of application that would make the CIA drool, but once again, private industry has beaten the public sector to the punch.

Guilty Firms Deny Responsibility

It is difficult to determine which applications are or have been bundled with VX2, due to the frequency of freeware updates and the program's inherently insidious nature. Companies that use VX2 are obviously tight lipped about it; companies who no longer use it, but once did, are in no rush to inform users that they were being spied on. Because of the nature of VX2's operation, however, these once-guilty firms still have a responsibility to inform their users. This spyware embeds itself into a user's hard drive; therefore, the application once bundled with VX2 does not even have to be running for it to gather information and send it to an ad server. Even if a company no longer maintains a relationship with VX2, unless it alerts its users to VX2's existence, and how to effectively delete it from their hard drive, the program will continue to do its dirty work. By keeping quiet, under the guise of not alarming their users, these firms remain co-conspirators in VX2's quest to snoop on the Web-browsing public.

The most popular application known to have used VX2 is the Audio Galaxy Satellite, a music-downloading application similar to Napster. Portal of Evil, a Web site that collects pages "from the margins of society," and one of the first sites to break the whole sordid VX2 story, has attempted to make Audio Galaxy accountable for bundling VX2 along with their Satellite freeware. In responses to both Portal of Evil and Wired.com, Audio Galaxy merely stated that VX2 was no longer included with their freeware, refusing to state when it was and for how long. The company said it had little knowledge of the program's use and blamed its presence in their software on Onflow, a software company that supplied Audio Galaxy with advertising graphics enhancers. Onflow maintains that it had never heard of VX2 until it was alerted by Portal of Evil.

Ignorance is a poor excuse for what companies such as Audio Galaxy have unleashed on the Web. What is now crystal clear is this: many companies offering freeware attach add-ons to their software willy-nilly, presumably under the spell of sleazy marketers, not knowing or not caring what this software will do to its users. . . . (Audio Galaxy did not respond to this writer's request for comment.)

The origins of the program are incredibly murky, and fraught with . . . secrecy. . . . No one has ever taken responsibility for writing the code (or funding such). As is often the case with such spyware, the program was probably developed and tested by a third-party tech department far removed from whoever wields it now, and then funneled through several different subsidiaries of a large parent company, in order to throw any curious bloodhounds off the scent. . . .

Thanks to the venal efforts of these people, the Web remains a lawless place huddled on the edge of civilization, full of mustache twirling barkers who cruise for those easy marks just off the stagecoach. And since times are tighter these days, the stakes are higher, the con jobs meaner, the medicine show a lot less funny. In the current political climate, anything that threatens our privacy deserves a long hard look, and a long hard fight. Until a sheriff finally arrives—until everyone realizes how much we stand to lose and how soon it will happen—we must get used to the hustler's hello: one hand slapping us in the back and the other one reaching into our pockets.

Incidentally, VX2 happens to share a name with a component of a variety of nerve agent. This brand of biological weapon is ten times more powerful than other nerve agents, and is characterized by its oily texture and long half-life. Whether the spyware's nomenclature was a loving tribute or a dark coincidence remains to be seen.

2

Companies Use Personal Information to Help Customers

Debbie A. Cannon

Debbie A. Cannon is president of DAC Enterprises, a firm that specializes in database management and Internet marketing.

Modern technology allows corporations to learn many intimate details about the shopping and spending habits of their customers. This information can be used in a positive or negative fashion. With the cautious use of personal data, companies can provide customized and personalized services that can benefit customers—and enhance corporate profits. The relationship between marketers and customers is based on trust, and those who abuse privacy rights hurt not only their customers, but ultimately their corporate profitability.

Today, every information manager and technologist faces the challenge and added responsibility of safeguarding the corporation's greatest asset: customer trust.

Technology has advanced to a state where collection, enhancement, and aggregation of data are instantaneous. Corporations now have the technology to analyze the finest details about each customer. They can determine the most profitable clients and tailor their marketing messages accordingly. Information can be collaborated upon across the enterprise so the customer hears a single voice.

While this ability is a positive development for the corpo-

Debbie A. Cannon, "The Ethics of Database Marketing: Personalization and Database Marketing—If Done Correctly—Can Serve Both the Organization and the Customer," *The Information Management Journal*, vol. 36, May/June 2002. Copyright © 2002 by ARMA International. Reproduced by permission.

ration and means better services for the client, it also adds a level of anxiety if the aggregation is not performed correctly and appropriately. As personalization and data collection technologies become more advanced, the expectations of consumers are shifting rapidly. Customers' patience levels are getting shorter and shorter. Mistakes are not quickly forgiven.

> *// Corporations face the challenge of making appropriate information available at all customer touch points while protecting privacy at the same time. //*

Privacy and customer permission have become the cornerstone to customer trust. Most importantly, trust has become the cornerstone to a continuing relationship. A recent IMG Strategies study reported that "having basic permission and privacy policies (e.g., an opt-in policy) is becoming just the price of entry for marketers as opposed to the differentiator it used to be a year earlier."

Customer Relationship Management

Companies want to "know" their customers; customer relationship management (CRM) is the key to that knowledge. IDC Research estimated that the worldwide market for CRM applications would more than double between 2000 and 2005, from $6.23 billion to $14.04 billion. CRM, however, is more than technology, software, and hardware. The real essence of CRM is in the acronym itself: customer relationship management—the relationship between the customer and those who manage the dialogue with the customer.

The database has become the strategic enabler for developing and maintaining this relationship. The role of database management as the vehicle for customer interaction has become a central strategic issue that reaches far beyond technology. Establishing and maintaining customer trust must be consistent across all customers' touch points [contacts]. Each piece of information made available at the various interactions with the customer must be made available throughout the enterprise.

The capability and role of the database in marketing has

drastically changed in the last decade. In times past, organizations maintained numerous databases. Customer information was stored in accounting, customer service, service, shipping, sales, and marketing databases. Each of these contained information important to that department's function. Unfortunately, it was rare when even the account number was consistent across the various departments. To add to the complexity, the formats were not standardized, and access was limited. The customer was seen as fragmented pieces of information. It also was commonplace for customers to receive multiple pieces of correspondence about the same topic and to have to present information about their accounts each time they contacted the company.

The information age brought with it technology and innovation that enabled a blending of these diverse databases that provides companies a more complete picture of the customer.

Personalization

Personalization has emerged as one way to send the right message to the right person at the right time. Personalization brings with it the question of just how much information is too much. Corporations face the challenge of making appropriate information available at all customer touch points while protecting privacy at the same time. As a safeguard, sensitizing and training must occur at all levels of the organization. A company could have highly publicized privacy policies, but it only takes one bad interaction with a customer service representative to lose a customer.

> *Privacy advocates are up in arms, but most people still are more upset over what companies forget about them than what they remember.*

Although personalization and privacy seem to be in conflict, the bottom line is that personalization benefits all involved: company, customer, and supplier. It gives the company a way to serve the customer better. Better service means better customer retention. Commonly, a five percent increase in customer retention can translate into a 25- to 125-percent increase in company profitability. . . .

The customer gets products and services tailored to his or her preference. No longer do consumers have to provide information over and over to the companies they do business with. And suppliers can control their inventories and product development cycles.

> *Most people . . . do not mind revealing personal information if it is used to better serve their needs and makes their interaction with a given company more convenient.*

Author Bruce Kasanoff sums up the seeming inconsistency between service and privacy: "It is a strange time. Privacy advocates are up in arms, but most people still are more upset over what companies forget about them than what they remember."

There is no lack of creativity in the application of technology to customer services. Some of the most significant advances in CRM can be found in the travel industry. Airlines, for example, closely track passenger history and preferences to better serve customers. One airline, for example, has begun using flight information to have travelers' cars ready at valet parking when they return from a trip. Changes in flight information can be sent via e-mail to a personal digital assistant (PDA) or cellular phone. In the future, flight delays can be reported directly to a destination hotel.

Privacy and Business Strategy

Privacy has become a top-down business strategy. At executive levels, companies are introducing the new position of chief privacy officer (CPO). CPOs serve as a liaison between the corporation and consumer. They often have veto power over product launches, marketing campaigns or strategic partnerships that they feel would interfere with the privacy of customers, employees, or suppliers.

Due to the never-ending media coverage of the legal aspect of consumer privacy, people are more aware of the types of information being collected about them. Most people, however, do not mind revealing personal information if it is used to better serve their needs and makes their interaction with a given company more convenient. A recent study conducted by Ipsos-Reid, a research and polling firm, reported that 47 percent of adults aged 18 to 34 have visited health-related Web sites and provided personal information, and 42 percent of those 35 to 54 years old have done so. Several of the most popular information-gathering and distribution sites on the Web are actually those of state governments. The sites contain information on everything from local government rules and regulations to birth, death, adoption, and marriage records.

Use with Caution

Employees and employers must become the custodians of customer trust and protect the privacy of their customers. They must learn to think beyond the proverbial box about the implications of the process of collecting and using information. Some organizations, however, are still learning how to apply CRM techniques appropriately as well as effectively. A dental group, for example, decided to apply personalization and database marketing techniques to send reminder postcards to current clients. Each postcard was properly personalized with the client information, including the amount of money toward dental care that they still had available from their insurance provider. Although technology was applied effectively, recipients were not pleased to see their personal information printed on postcards that could be read by postal carriers and anyone else handling the mail.

The customer relationship is built on more than the pieces of data and collected history. Merely collecting data and storing it in data warehouses can be a tremendous waste of corporate resources. Personalization and database marketing—conducted correctly—serve both the organizations and the customers.

Business cultures must grasp the concept that every single point of contact within the organization and throughout the supply chain is a key to the success of customer relationships. Technology is merely the enabler. The application of the technology—based on understanding the impact each and every dialogue has on the total customer relationship—is quickly becoming the highest priority within corporations. Businesses no longer focus on product share alone. The shift has moved toward customer share. This trend shows no sign of slowing down.

3

Employee Privacy Rights Are Under Attack in the Workplace

Charles J. Sykes

Charles J. Sykes is a research fellow at the Hoover Institution, a conservative public policy research center devoted to the study of politics, economics, and international affairs.

Americans are denied the most basic rights to privacy at work. Employers can listen to phone conversations, read personal e-mails, browse through an employee's past employment records, and even demand bodily fluids for drug tests. If law enforcement agencies or other government authorities wanted to take such actions, they would be required first to obtain a court order from a judge. However, businesses need not follow such rules. Most workers spend about one-third of their lives at their place of employment, leaving their rights to privacy at home. Congress should make it a priority to enact legislation that guarantees privacy rights to employees in the workplace.

Perhaps you have had the famous Freudian dream, in which you suddenly realize that you have gone to school or work, but have forgotten to get dressed. Whatever the classic analysis might be, the dream is a stark metaphor for the modern American workplace. Many of us are naked, at least in the sense that we have few protections of our privacy. On some occasions, workers find the metaphor to be literally true: some employers

Charles J. Sykes, *The End of Privacy*. New York: St. Martin's Press, 1999. Copyright © 1999 by Charles J. Sykes. Reproduced by permission of St. Martin's Press LLC.

have installed video cameras in locker rooms and restrooms, a practice that is legal in all but a handful of states. But the invasions of employee privacy are actually far more widespread and intrusive. No federal law makes it illegal for an employer to gather and compile highly personal information about employees, even if it is unrelated to the job they do. It is perfectly legal for your boss to monitor your family life, check up on the organizations you belong to, delve into your medical history, and even do background checks on your personality traits and education.

- Employers can listen in to your phone calls.
- They can read your e-mail—even if your message is marked "private."
- They can listen in to your voice mail.
- They can monitor what is on the screen of your computer and what you have left on your hard drive.
- They can install software that monitors the number of keystrokes you perform per hour, and measures the time you are away from your workstation.
- They can make you urinate into a cup to test for drugs.
- They can read your credit reports, and look at your medical records.
- They cannot give you a polygraph test, but they can probe your innermost thoughts with psychological tests.
- They can share information about you with creditors and government agents.

The violations, however, are not all one-way. Disgruntled employees have been known to wear concealed wires or hidden recorders to tape conversations and meetings with coworkers and managers. One San Francisco employment lawyer estimates that as many as one-fifth of his clients tell him that they have secretly recorded conversations in their offices. Even though many of these tape recordings violate state laws, some judges appear to overlook the invasions and have allowed aggrieved workers to introduce the tapes as evidence. Ironically, new developments in employment law have actually helped shape the current climate of mistrust. Because of the rising tide of litigiousness, employers have a limited ability to get honest and thorough information about employees from past employers (a negative letter of recommendation is an invitation to a lawsuit). They may also be forbidden by law to ask about certain problem areas in an applicant's past—including arrests. An unintended consequence of such protections has been that employers have become subtler, more creative, and more roundabout in their approach to learning about their employees.

Strictly speaking, the tradition of delving into the private lives of employees is not new in American business. In its early years [1910s], the Ford Motor Company pioneered corporate paternalism by scrutinizing the home life and personal finances of its employees to determine if they were worthy to receive profit-sharing bonuses. Representatives of Henry Ford's "Sociological Department" visited homes of employees to determine whether they gambled, drank, had dirty homes, an unwholesome diet, or sent money to foreign relatives. Following in his footsteps, business continues to argue that its ability to probe into the background of employees is both a fundamental right and a business necessity.

Federal law provides little protection to employees for several reasons: first, though public employees enjoy some minimal Fourth Amendment protections, those rights do not extend to the private sector. Second, Congress has been reluctant to enact privacy rules for private businesses, even going so far as exempting employers from laws protecting the confidentiality of electronic communications. "When most Americans go to work in the morning, they might just as well be going to a foreign country," says Lewis Maltby, of the ACLU [American Civil Liberties Union], Workplace Rights Project, "because they are equally beyond the reach of the Constitution in both situations. And unfortunately, federal law does very, very little to fill this void."

How Widespread Are Such Practices?

One survey found that two-thirds of the nation's largest corporations hire private investigators to gather information about employees' private lives. Another recent poll of 906 large and midsize employers found that more than one-third of them conduct one or more kinds of electronic surveillance on their employees. If any kind of electronic monitoring is included—including the number of keystrokes by data-entry workers, phone logs, and videotaping to deter crime—the proportion rose to 63.4 percent. In 1993, *MacWorld* magazine estimated that 20 million workers were being monitored through computers on their desktops. A widely publicized survey of eighty-seven Fortune 500 companies with a combined 3.2 million employees found that 75 percent said they collected information about employees beyond what workers voluntarily provide and almost half did do so without informing the employees. More than two-thirds reported hiring private investigators to do background checks of their workers; more than one-third (35 percent) said they used medical records to make decisions about employees. The vast majority acknowledged that they shared information about their employees with government agencies and creditors.

New technologies promise even more sophisticated workplace monitoring. A Virginia company is now marketing artificial intelligence software that automatically scans employees' e-mail for "offensive language." A New Jersey company has developed a system to monitor whether employees at their restaurant wash their hands after going to the bathroom. Given trends in litigation employment law—which hold employers liable for everything from employee honesty to sexual harassment—the level of intrusiveness is likely to keep rising.

You've Got Mail

One of the cases that underlined the vulnerability of employees and the lack of legal protections was *Shoars* v. *Epson America, Inc.* [1994]. Like many American companies, Epson had an extensive e-mail system, which was administered by a woman named Alana Shoars. Feeling that confidentiality was essential to the new network, Shoars assured her colleagues at Epson that the company's e-mail system was private and their passwords and communications secure.

They were not.

When Shoars discovered that one of the company's executives was eavesdropping on electronic messages, she confronted him—and was promptly fired. Because the incident occurred in California, Shoars had high hopes that California's constitutional protections of privacy gave her an advantage when she sued Epson for wrongful discharge, slander, and for invasion of privacy. But Epson, like other employers, insisted that since the company owned the e-mail system, it had the right to control it and to monitor how it was used. Since the company provided the equipment, the software, and the network, they reserved the right to ensure that their employees used electronic mail strictly for business purposes.

Privacy activists like Philip R. Zimmerman, the legendary creator of PGP (which stands for Pretty Good Privacy), an encryption system, challenge the argument that because companies own equipment, they should have the right to control and monitor its contents. "I use a company pen," says Zimmerman. "If I use it to write a letter to my wife, does that mean they can read the letter?" But that was precisely what Epson was claiming. As it turned out, there was no California law protecting the privacy of e-mail. Shoars tried to argue that the violation of e-mail privacy was covered under the state's older laws dealing with wiretapping, but the trial court rejected her argument. The court also rejected her argument that Epson's snooping violated California's broader constitutional right of privacy. In a setback for the privacy rights of the state's employees, the court ruled that the constitutional right of privacy only protected *personal* information. The court saw no reason to extend privacy protections to "business-oriented communications." Nor did federal law provide any help. When Congress passed the Electronic and Communications Privacy Act to cover e-mail communication in 1986, it explicitly exempted employers. Thus, even though Shoars felt she had a sound commonsense basis for her case—Epson's promises of confidentiality, the use of passwords that seemed to promise privacy—Epson's snooping was protected by law.

> *When most Americans go to work in the morning, they might just as well be going to a foreign country . . . because they are equally beyond the reach of the Constitution.*

Indeed, the U.S. Supreme Court has granted employers a good deal of leeway in their prying into employee activities. In 1987, the Court ruled in favor of a supervisor in a public-sector workplace who searched one of his employee's files, office, and desk, ruling that the worker had no reasonable expectation of privacy at his workplace. Since public employees have greater constitutional protections against unreasonable searches and seizures than workers in the private sector, the clear implication of the ruling was that private companies had been granted even broader license to search employees' work areas and communications. . . .

A study by the Society for Human Resource Management

found that 80 percent of the organizations surveyed used e-mail, but only 36 percent had policies for its use, and only 32 percent had written privacy rules. That may be changing, as more companies begin to protect themselves by explicitly informing employees that their e-mail may be subject to surveillance. Such surveillance is also likely to become even more aggressive, especially given the aggressiveness of litigators who not only subpoena every piece of document and piece of paper, but have also learned that deleted e-mails can be accessed and used against companies at trial. Chevron, for example, had to pay $2.2 million to four women in a case that involved offensive e-mail and interoffice mail. Among other things, the company found itself liable for some of its employees using the e-mail to transmit documents like "25 Reasons Why Beer Is Better Than Women."

The No-Privacy Zone

In the 1970s Congress created the Federal Privacy Commission, which studied the issue of employee privacy in depth. Business groups lobbied the commission against recommending federal legal protections, insisting that they should be allowed to develop their own voluntary policies to protect employees from privacy abuses. Commission Chairman David Linowes, a professor at the University of Illinois, has conducted follow-up studies to determine how well business has done in protecting privacy. His conclusion is that voluntary regulation has been a dismal failure. Not only do businesses continue to collect detailed and highly personal information, but they often also fail to ensure the accuracy or the confidentiality of those files.

"The amount of unsubstantiated and irrelevant information that finds its way into files is amazing," complained Linowes. "Rumors, poison-pen letters, things that appeared in newspapers. We found many errors that resulted in terrible abuse. Employees should be allowed to correct errors, but 24 percent of companies do not allow corrections."

Employees under review or who are being considered for promotions might come under special scrutiny, which might include attempts to learn more about their character, past behavior, spending habits, friends, and associates. In one case found by Linowes, a man had been denied promotion because his file described him as "known to have used drugs." It later turned out that one of his neighbors had told company investigators that he had "heard" he had once tried marijuana. Another woman's personnel file included grade-school report cards and evaluations from her third-grade teacher, including a note describing the woman's mother as "crazy." That note reportedly led her employer to question her mental soundness. Another executive's file included his complete medical records, including the fact that he had complained to his doctor about recurrent headaches. A scribbled notation that the man "seems to have difficulty managing finances" may have cost him a promotion to a job supervising company budgets.

Covert Lab Tests

At the Lawrence Berkeley Laboratory, which is operated jointly by state and federal agencies, employees were routinely tested—without their knowledge—for a variety of traits, ailments, and conditions. Black employees were tested for the sickle-cell trait; female employees were tested for pregnancy. Other employees were routinely tested for syphilis, without ever being told the tests were being conducted or informed of the results. The lab defended its practices by arguing that the tests were simply part of its general mandatory medical examination. Because employees were also asked to fill out a questionnaire that asked questions about venereal disease and menstrual problems, the laboratory argued, the employees should have expected that they might also be tested for such problems.

> *The amount of unsubstantiated and irrelevant information that finds its way into files is amazing. . . . Rumors, poison-pen letters, things that appeared in newspapers.*

Although a federal district judge threw out the case, the Ninth District Court of Appeals reversed the decision, ruling that the procedures violated both the federal and California privacy rights of the employees. "One can think of few subject areas more personal and more likely to implicate privacy interest than that of one's health or genetic makeup," the court ruled. "[I]t goes without saying that the most basic violation possible involved the performance of unauthorized tests—that is, the nonconsensual retrieval of previously unrevealed medical information that may be unknown even to the plaintiffs." In particular, the tests for syphilis and pregnancy were "highly sensitive, even relative to other medical information." The Appeals Court also rejected the claim that filling out the questionnaire had given the laboratory the go-ahead for the other tests. "The fact that plaintiffs acquiesced in the minor intrusion of checking or not checking three boxes on a questionnaire doesn't mean that they had reason to expect further intrusions in the form of having their blood and urine tested for specific conditions that correspond tangentially if at all to the written questions." (The court pointed out that pregnancy is neither a "venereal disease" nor a "menstrual disorder.")

> **❝ The same action that would be deemed an unconstitutional violation of your rights when done by the government, is perfectly permissible if done by your boss. ❞**

Although the Lawrence case may be an extreme example, Linowes found that 38 percent of the companies surveyed do not inform employees of types of records maintained on them; 44 percent do not tell personnel how records are used; and nearly 60 percent fail to inform employees about their policies of providing information to the government. Besides that, 18 percent don't tell their employees what records they can see and 42 percent have no policy for conducting periodic reviews of their record-keeping system. He was also troubled by the lack of solid policies to correct recurrent errors in the dossiers. Nearly one out of four companies (23 percent) had no policy to forward corrections to anyone who received incorrect information within the past two years. "With information being transmitted across the country and abroad at the speed of light," noted Linowes, "an error in one record can be propagated a hundredfold instantaneously. If no effort is made to forward a correction, this is detrimental to both the recipient organization and the individual."

One of the few recommendations of the Privacy Commission that did result in federal legislation was the proposal to limit the use of polygraphs by private employers. By 1987, employers were administering nearly 2 million polygraph tests a year to applicants, using the procedures to probe into their religious, political beliefs, sex lives, and union affiliations. In response, Congress passed the Employee Polygraph Protection Act, which bars the use of lie detectors to screen new hires. (Although businesses can still employ lie detectors on their workers if they have a "reasonable suspicion" of wrongdoing.) . . .

The Legal Right to Invade Privacy

For many employees, the most obvious and direct challenge to their privacy comes in the form of drug tests. One of the paradoxes of privacy protection is the way the courts have applied the Fourth Amendment's protections against unreasonable search and seizure. An individual's home is protected against entry by any government agent. Those agents cannot seize his property or papers without an express court order. Courts have ruled repeatedly that the Constitution does not merely protect places, but also people, and thus the Fourth Amendment's protections also apply to any other invasive proceedings, including strip searches. Private entities have even less access than the government to a man's home and person; under almost every circumstance, the entry of a private home or the intrusion into a person's physical security by a private citizen is a crime. Although there are procedures for intrusive disclosures through the discovery process in a civil trial, no one except the government has a right to invade the privacy of the home—and even then, the right is tightly circumscribed.

But in the area of workplace law, the equation is turned on its head. In most contexts, private employers have far more power than the government to violate the privacy of their workers. Put another way, an individual is protected more effectively from the government than from his employer because the protection against warrantless searches does not extend to the private sector. The result is that the same action that would be deemed an unconstitutional violation of your rights when done by the government, is perfectly permissible if done by your boss—including wiretapping, reading your private e-mails, and drug testing.

The courts have repeatedly found that drug tests are a significant invasion of privacy, violating not only the Fourth Amendment, but also the Fifth Amendment's protection against self-incrimination, and the Fourteenth Amendment's protection of due process and privacy. Because those protections are not absolute, some forms of testing have been upheld, including those in which there is a "reasonable suspicion" that someone has been under the influence of drugs. Another exception is for random testing of government employees in jobs involving the public safety, and of some student athletes.

In general, though, the courts have ruled out blanket or random drug tests without any reasonable justification. "By analogy," [legal analyst] Judith Decew writes, "although United States banks are surely concerned to ensure that their employees are not embezzlers, that worry does not entitle them to search all bank employees and their homes on the chance that they may uncover a dishonest employee." But since the constitutional protections against unreasonable searches do not extend to private businesses, employers *are* able to search the urine and blood of their employees on the chance they may be using drugs.

> *If society respects and values privacy, can it tolerate a situation that denies any privacy protections for the place where we spend one-third of our lives?*

For many workers the requirement that they submit to drug tests is the most obvious and direct challenge to their privacy. One study found that 80 percent of the companies in the survey tested their employees for drugs, and millions of Americans are required to urinate into cups, jars, and bottles every year as a condition of their employment. Although Supreme Court Justice Antonin Scalia has called drug testing a "needless indignity," it has widespread support and illustrates the problems of balancing privacy concerns with other priorities. Supporters of drug testing point to the overwhelming evidence that drug use not only exacts a societal cost, but also hurts the productivity of American business. Recent government estimates put the cost of drug abuse to the nation's employers at $60 to $100 billion a year in property damage, absenteeism and tardiness, reduced productivity and quality, higher costs for health insurance and worker's compensation, employee theft, and the turnover of workers. Many of the nation's largest and most prestigious corporations require pre-employment tests; the list includes more than one-quarter of the Fortune 500 corporations and such trendsetters as the *New York Times*, IBM, Exxon, Federal Express, AT&T, and Lockheed. Obviously, the most compelling justifications of drug testing involve jobs that affect safety, such as railway workers and airline pilots. But the vast majority of people tested are not in the classic "safety-sensitive" jobs.

What no one seriously questions, though, is the fact that drug tests involve a considerable loss of privacy, ranging from puncturing the skin to obtain blood to actually watching a person give a urine sample (in order to ensure that nothing is substituted). Beyond the physical intrusion, drug tests may reveal a good deal more medical information about the person subjected to such tests. Judith Decew notes that such tests can reveal information about the person's use of birth-control, pregnancy, epilepsy, manic-depression, diabetes, heart disease, even schizophrenia medications. In addition, it is also not always clear who has access to the results of such tests. Nor is it obvious that the tests—upon which so much rides for an individual in terms of employment, insurance, and reputation—are all that accurate.[1] . . .

Working for Privacy

The transparent workplace raises several nagging issues for privacy rights: If society respects and values privacy, can it tolerate a situation that denies any privacy protections for the place where we spend one-third of our lives? Can we pretend that we can still have privacy if we have no right to protect ourselves against violations by people who have economic power over us? For most American workers a choice of their privacy or their livelihood is no choice at all.

Employers are not bound by the same constitutional limit as government; the Bill of Rights was created to restrict the powers of government, not the powers of private citizens. But even so, constitutional protections of privacy/information rights are not irrelevant. Infringements of privacy by an employer necessarily affect those rights vis-à-vis the rest of society. When it comes to information, the walls between private and

1. Critics claim that many of the drug tests have error rates as high as 60 percent. Moreover, the tests cannot determine whether a worker is actually under the influence of a drug at the time, nor do they measure how any specific drug might impair a person's performance.

public are increasingly porous. Given the fluid nature of information, what good are our protections against government intrusion if employers are given carte blanche to probe our lives and share that information with those same governmental agencies? It is also important to remember that employers have not resorted to draconian surveillance techniques out of sheer ill will. Rather, businesses can make a compelling case that the current legal climate gives them little choice whether or not to monitor their employees. Society's penchant for litigiousness has forced companies to assume a defensive posture. Over the last several decades, the trend has been toward creating new classes of legal actions that customers, partners, and workers can bring against companies. Not only do they face a raft of potential lawsuits and complaints from employees—for discrimination, for sexual harassment, for unfairness of every sort—but they also find themselves held liable for their employees' conduct and action. Such laws make it difficult to dismiss problem employees, and give businesses powerful incentives for ever-increasing levels of surveillance, if only for self-preservation. From a practical point of view, any protections of employee privacy may have to be counterbalanced by shifting more responsibility from companies to individual employees.

Legislation should probably begin with the most egregious violations, including electronic monitoring, video surveillance, and medical information. At minimum, companies should be encouraged to adopt the so-called fair-information practices. This would mean that personal information be used only for the specific purpose for which it was gathered; that employees be able to see information about themselves; and they should be given a chance to correct any incorrect information that might be in their files.

But there are definite limits to the power of legislation. More hopeful, however, might be changes in the marketplace itself, as companies begin to use privacy policies to compete for customers and employees. Increasingly, businesses will find that protecting employee privacy is not only an attractive option for employees, but gives those employers with the strongest assurances a clear competitive advantage. Just as customers will gravitate toward merchants who prove reliable and trustworthy in handling their data, so valued employees will be attracted to environments that promise to treat them with respect and reticence.

4

Corporate Security Depends on the Monitoring of Workers

Robin L. Wakefield

Robin L. Wakefield is a certified public accountant and an assistant professor of information systems management at Baylor University in Texas.

Corporate managers have the legal right and moral responsibility to monitor the use of company computers, e-mail, and other electronic systems. Employees abuse these networks in a myriad of ways, including surfing the Internet during work hours and stealing company secrets. In several cases in which workers used their employers' computers to send harassing or pornographic e-mails, victims filed multimillion-dollar lawsuits against the companies. While too much surveillance can hurt morale, a clearly stated company policy that details monitoring strategies can benefit both workers and the company. It is the duty of managers to detect, investigate, and report any abuses that take place on company time and property.

Information security and employee privacy are important issues facing all organizations. E-mail monitoring software will grow significantly in the next five years, from $139 million in sales (2001) to $662 million (2006), according to International Data Corp. (IDC). Federal legislation mandates that companies actively safeguard personal information. Standards established by the Federal Trade Commission (FTC) focus on maintaining

Robin L. Wakefield, "Computer Monitoring and Surveillance: Balancing Privacy with Security," *The CPA Journal*, vol. 74, July 2004. Copyright © 2004 by New York Society of Certified Public Accountants. Reproduced by permission.

the security and confidentiality of personal records and information, protecting against internal and external threats to the security or integrity of such records, and protecting against unauthorized access or use of personal records.

Whereas past information security efforts centered on protecting systems from external threats (e.g., computer hackers), the risk of internal threats to personal information has spawned both new legislation and new market opportunities. Content and information security services is a burgeoning market that IDC predicts will exceed $23.5 billion by 2007, with a yearly growth rate of 20.9%. . . .

> *In one recent incident . . . a sexual harassment suit cost Chevron $2.2 million because an employee sent coarse messages over the company e-mail system.*

Content security involves using electronic means to monitor the transmission and storage of data over a company's network. Content-filtering software can stop spam, scan attachments for inappropriate language, block dangerous attachments, stop intellectual property breaches, quarantine questionable messages or embedded images, and notify systems managers when policies are violated. The potential costs of litigation from adverse network practices underscore the importance of content security. Thomas Shumaker II, an expert in labor and employment law, believes that "CPAs [certified public accountants] have a duty to take reasonable steps to protect both their employees and their clients. Don't be afraid to monitor the workplace." Shumaker thinks it is critical for companies to realize that they are legally liable for all transmissions within their networks. In one recent incident, reported by *The New York Times*, a sexual harassment suit cost Chevron $2.2 million because an employee sent coarse messages over the company e-mail system.

Employee monitoring is one component of [accounting firm] BDO Seidman LLP's critical antifraud procedures (CAP) program. Carl Pergola, national director of BDO's CAP, states that "it is essential for organizations to monitor employees" in order to comply with federal mandates such as the Gramm-Leach-Bliley Act [which provides protection against the sale of personal financial information]. The content security approach of their CAP program recommends monitoring servers, backups, e-mail, and Internet activity, as well as conducting random computer forensics on employee computers. Pergola acknowledges that employee surveillance and monitoring is only one part of a comprehensive program that may also include background investigations, interviews, and fraud education.

Developing an information security strategy that involves employee monitoring requires that the information risks and system controls of an entity are understood. Any strategy requires the implementation of surveillance tools and the development of a monitoring policy that effectively reduces risk and demonstrates compliance with federal laws. A comprehensive content security policy focuses on four areas tailored to the needs, resources, and goals of individual organizations: prevention, detection, investigation, and reporting.

Prevention

Prevention is the main component of an information security strategy. It includes a clearly written and really available corporate policy that defines information security principles, establishes acceptable and unacceptable practices, outlines criminal offenses, and describes disciplinary actions.

Monitoring is an effective deterrent and detection technique within an overall content security strategy. Prior court rulings suggest that reasonableness is an important standard of acceptable monitoring activities. Electronic monitoring is reasonable when there is a business purpose, when policies exist to set the privacy expectations of employees, and when employees are informed of the rules and understand the means used to monitor the workplace.

One important component of prevention is establishing the business purposes of monitoring, which may include the following:

• Preventing misuse of resources. Companies can discourage unproductive personal activities such as online shopping or web surfing on company time. Monitoring employee performance is one way to reduce unnecessary network traffic and reduce the consumption of network bandwidth.

• Promoting adherence to policies. Online surveillance is one means of verifying employee observance of company networking policies.

• Preventing lawsuits. Firms can be held liable for discrimination or employee harassment in the workplace. Organizations can also be involved in infringement suits through employees that distribute copyrighted material over corporate networks.

• Safeguarding records. Federal legislation requires organizations to protect personal information. Monitoring can determine the extent of compliance with company policies and programs overseeing information security. Monitoring may also deter unlawful appropriation of personal information, and potential spam or viruses.

• Safeguarding company assets. The protection of intellectual property, trade secrets, and business strategies is a major concern. The ease of information transmission and storage makes it imperative to monitor employee actions as part of a broader policy.

> **Software tools can retrieve employee e-mail, restrict access to Internet sites, record keystrokes, and randomly access employee computer screens.**

A second component of prevention is determining the ownership of technology resources. The ownership of the firm's networks, servers, computers, files, and e-mail should be explicitly stated. There should be a distinction between an employee's personal electronic devices, which should be limited and proscribed, and those owned by the firm.

Establishing ownership reduces employees' expectations of privacy and solidifies the employer's rights. Courts have consistently favored employers' rights to protect their interests given that the work is done at the employer's place of business, the employer owns the equipment, the employer has an interest in monitoring employee activity to ensure the quality of work, and the employer has the right to protect property from theft and fraud.

The acceptable and unacceptable uses of company networks should be clearly described. Boundaries should be set for the personal use of e-mail, the Internet, and downloads. A company should explicitly define what kinds of language, copyrighted material, or images are prohibited from being transmitted over, or accessed via, company networks.

Finally, employees should be educated about the reasons behind information security, including employer and employee protection, relevant legislation, expectations of compliance, and potential consequences. They should also be informed of the specific types of surveillance activities used and how they will affect workflow. Employees should be required to sign a statement agreeing to the specific monitoring activities related to their work and equipment.

Pergola recommends that employers tell employees that monitoring will take place throughout their employment, that it will be random, and that compliance is mandatory. Pergola says that knowledge is key to keeping employees satisfied and productive in a monitored environment. Clearly stating monitoring intentions and obtaining prior consent is essential to minimize invasion-of-privacy claims.

Shumaker also advises that employers reduce privacy expectations by posting their right to monitor the workplace in company handbooks and personnel policies. He says. "It is important for employers to demonstrate that monitoring is a routine and known activity in the organization." Companies are at greater risk when their policies are silent on the issue.

Detection

Detection is an integral part of a content security policy. It involves implementing monitoring methods that effectively reduce risk. Software tools can retrieve employee e-mail, restrict access to Internet sites, record keystrokes, and randomly access employee computer screens. Other tools can screen network transmissions for prohibited words, phrases, or images. Monitoring activities can also be outsourced to a third party.

Well-devised monitoring techniques should detect security breaches as soon as possible. Network controls, supported by company policies, protect both employees and clients and set a tone that conveys organizational responsibility and respect for others.

Investigation

The third area of a content security policy is investigation. The following are important steps in investigating a potential security violation:

• Establish an information security officer or response team to investigate security lapses.

• Develop a plan to obtain legal advice when possible criminal offenses are discovered.

• Prescribe the course of action for different kinds of security violations. Actions might include interviews, collection of evidence, formal reports, or legal conferences.

• Describe the consequences for each level of security breach.

• Determine when police intervention is necessary.

• Establish safeguards to protect employees who raise concerns in good faith.

• Use discretion when addressing anonymous allegations. Weigh the seriousness of the issue and the likelihood of confirming the allegation from credible sources.

Reporting

The final area to address in a content security policy is reporting. A designated security officer or response team should provide formal reports on security breaches, as well as on the actions taken, to the appropriate executive or committee for review. The effectiveness of disciplinary or legal consequences and of the monitoring controls should be evaluated. Information security efforts should be coordinated with the company's internal audit department.

Reducing Risk, Improving Compliance

Information security services is one of the most active areas of the IT [information technology] services industry. IDC believes that the number-one issue for businesses over the next five years will be compliance with legislative requirements to protect information. Pergola predicts that "as the responsibility for fraud is more clearly defined, surveillance activities and other anti-fraud procedures will only increase." Information security strategies, including network surveillance, will be the principal focus of companies seeking to reduce risk and demonstrate compliance.

5

Federal Law Violates Medical Privacy

Peter Byrne

Peter Byrne is a journalist who writes articles for SF Weekly.

The Bush administration claims that the privacy rights of medical patients are protected by the recently instated law, the Health Insurance Portability and Accountability Act (HIPAA). This claim is contrary to a provision in the act that grants law enforcement authorities unlimited access to medical records under the guise of fighting terrorism. HIPAA allows local police, the FBI, the Central Intelligence Agency, and even secret agents within the Defense Department to obtain a person's medical and psychiatric records without court orders, warrants, or explanations about the target of the investigation. Although this little-publicized provision of HIPAA is ignored by those who defend the act, it is a stunning threat to personal privacy rights. Unless Congress repeals this provision of HIPAA, America's national security agencies and government snoops will have unlimited power to investigate the most private and personal records of millions of citizens.

In early April [2003], my dentist was rooting around inside my mouth, making the terrible jokes for which he is infamous while I, as usual, laughed politely. Then he wiped his hands clean and handed me a toothbrush and a "Notice of Privacy Practices," which he asked me to sign. I skimmed through it until I got to a part that said my medical records can be dis-

Peter Byrne, "Big Doctor Is Watching; as of April 14, the National Security Police Can Monitor Your Medical Records Without Your Knowledge. So Can the Local Police," *SF Weekly*, May 28, 2003. Copyright © 2004 by New Times, Inc. All rights reserved. Reproduced by permission.

closed for "essential government functions," including "law enforcement, execution of a military mission, conducting intelligence, counterintelligence, and national security activities." My newly shining molars nearly fell out of my face.

According to the six-page privacy notice, the details of my checkered medical (and psychiatric) history are now open to people I do not trust, including my employer, insurance salesmen, HMO [health maintenance organization] executives, bill collectors, Walgreens clerks, steak fajita-eaters, and the spies with nests inside the Federal Building. . . .

Like many San Franciscans, I've expressed myself politically over the years in ways that (my suspicious mind has always assumed) might draw some measure of governmental notice. Somehow, though, it's more unsettling to think that the FBI might have a file on my weird bumps, adverse reactions, poxes, rashes, major medical events, psychic abrasions, and infected pimples, too. And it could.

As of April 14 [2003], physicians, dentists, therapists, health maintenance organizations, and insurance companies are required by federal law to tell patients that their medical records—long considered private and available to the government only if it showed a judge probable cause that a law had been violated—can be scooped up by the FBI, the CIA, state troopers, or even the local police, on the spot, as a result of a simple, oral request. The new law, called the Health Insurance Portability and Accountability Act Privacy Rule (HIPAA), is being promoted by the Bush administration as an act of privacy protection.

> **//** *Medical records can be disclosed for 'essential government functions,' including 'law enforcement, execution of a military mission, conducting intelligence, counterintelligence, and national security activities.'* **//**

In important ways that have gained little publicity, however, HIPAA vastly decreases the privacy privileges traditionally afforded to medical records, and organizations on the political left and right—from the American Civil Liberties Union to the Heritage Foundation—are united in their opposition to the new law. They contend that HIPAA requires doctors to violate the Hippocratic oath, the ethical code that has governed the confidentiality of the physician-patient relationship since the days of the ancient Greeks; that it strips patients of any meaningful control over their medical records; and that it increases the investigatory powers of federal, state, and local police agencies in violation of the Constitution's prohibition against warrantless searches.

Psychiatrists are suing the federal government to limit HIPAA's reach; there are several bills pending in Congress to repeal or rewrite it. Hundreds of thousands of California retirees are trying to stop HIPAA dead in its tracks. In San Francisco, a key city official is prepared to defy any law enforcement official who comes snooping around City Hall for personal medical information without a search warrant.

At the same time, though, state officials in Sacramento have written a bill to weaken California's strong privacy laws in favor of the far more invasive law enforcement privileges of HIPAA. And until something changes on the HIPAA front, you will probably never know if police agents decide to comb through your family's intimate medical information on the basis of an unwarranted suspicion and a simple verbal request.

Weakened Privacy Standards

The foundation of medical ethics is contained in the Oath of Hippocrates, which says, in part, "All that may come to my knowledge in the exercise of my profession, which ought not to be spread abroad, I will keep secret and never reveal." The power of the oath has kept medical records largely confidential through the centuries in societies built on slavery, feudalism, and industrial capitalism.

Our world is, of course, more complex than ancient Greece. Studies show that in the age of computerized record-keeping, as many as 150 people, including neurosurgeons, pharmacists, billing clerks, and janitors, are privy to the contents of a hospital patient's chart. Now, the Hippocratic oath may be rendered essentially meaningless by a combination of federal law and the Information Age's propensity to create ever larger medical databases for reasons of efficiency, profit, and social control.

Until the mid-1990s, federal laws on medical privacy applied only to federal agencies, intending to limit possible misuse of this sensitive information for political purposes. Still, medical records were largely presumed to be private, and that presumption was backed by state statutes and the common law traditions.

But in 1996, Congress passed the Health Insurance Portability and Accountability Act, sponsored by Sens. Edward Kennedy (D-Mass.) and Nancy Kassebaum (R-Kan.). This legislation was intended to make health insurance portable for people who changed jobs. It required the government to develop guidelines for the secure transmission of electronic medical data. It called for the creation of a national standard for protecting the privacy of personal medical records.

Responsibility for writing the details for the implementation of HIPAA fell to officials at the U.S. Department of Health and Human Services. They were intensely lobbied by hospital and medical groups, HMOs, privacy rights advocates, pharmaceutical companies, medical equipment suppliers, software manufacturers, and law enforcement agencies. In the end, the law did not fully satisfy any particular interest groups (except, perhaps, law enforcement and intelligence agencies). Most medical providers were allowed more than two years to fully comply with the regulation's labyrinth of bureaucratic requirements, which includes training a HIPAA specialist inside every medical organization and practice.

> *Anyone from a national security agency can walk into a doctor's office and say, 'This is a national security issue. Turn over the record.'*

HIPAA governs the privacy activities of all professionals who transmit medical and billing data electronically—which includes just about every medical professional, as well as group health plans and companies that handle financial and billing matters for providers. It also covers networks of lawyers, accountants, consultants, and pharmacists associated with health plans and doctors. Under HIPAA, patients cannot prevent their electronic and paper records from being used by any of these groups for health delivery and payment purposes, and some direct marketing is allowed. The medical industry is expected to police itself for unauthorized uses of patient information; the penalty for noncompliance is $100 per occurrence.

But controversial portions of the new law and its associated regulations allow police and intelligence agencies to obtain medical dossiers on demand, and to order medical-record custodians not to inform patients that the government has looked at their records.

Richard Campanelli, director of the Office of Civil Rights of the Department of Health and Human Services, which enforces HIPAA, says that the new law "limits access to medical records for the first time." For example, Campanelli notes, before April 14 there were no federal laws guiding local law enforcement access to medical records. Likewise, he draws attention to nittygritty details of HIPAA, such as a requirement that doctors must allow patients to correct errors in their medical records, and another that computer screens must be turned away from prying eyes in the waiting room.

Clearly, though, Campanelli emphasizes portions of the new law that strengthen medical privacy in particular cases and underplays those aspects of the law that weaken medical privacy on a sweeping basis.

No Limits on Law Enforcement

Robert Gellman, a Washington, D.C.–based privacy lawyer who was deeply involved in the HIPAA drafting process as a congressional staff member, points out that before HIPAA, patients routinely consented to allowing their doctor to share their medical records with colleagues and business support people. That is not the part of HIPAA that bothers him.

"The law enforcement portion of HIPAA is its single worst feature," Gellman remarks. "[To get medical records] a government official can wave a badge and say, 'I qualify under HIPAA.' There are no requirements for warrants, court orders, subpoenas, or probable cause. Anyone from a national security agency can walk into a doctor's office and say, 'This is a national security issue. Turn over the record.' It would allow an HMO to hand over its entire database upon request."

HIPAA regulates organizations that create medical records, attempting to provide rules for all categories of possible disclosure of medical information. In most situations, HIPAA gives the patient zero control over who sees his records; medical-record holders, on the other hand, have tremendous leeway to allow government authorities to search and seize doctors' records for research, public health, criminal investigation, and intelligence-gathering purposes.

For years, the FBI and other federal agencies have been performing end runs around federal laws that prohibited them from spying on Americans by purchasing personal information from consumer information databanks. Huge databases of medical information—obtained from divorce filings, police reports, DMV records, bank account statements, and credit card charges for purchases of prosthetic limbs, coronary drugs, birth control devices, enemas, and so on—are gathered and stored by data aggregation firms that are in the business of selling consumer information. One such firm, ChoicePoint, has dozens of service contracts with federal agencies, including the FBI and the Department of Homeland Security, for access to the company's trove of 17 billion records.

But a wide variety of legal scholars and medical professionals interviewed for this story say the enhanced powers granted to law enforcement by HIPAA herald a fundamental change in the body of law governing the use and disclosure of medical and psychiatric records. One part of HIPAA empowers local police, sheriffs, county and city attorneys, district attorneys, state attorneys general, and federal crime-stoppers to obtain medical records under weakened standards. Another section similarly empowers the intelligence community, including the National Security Agency, the FBI, the CIA, the State Department, the Department of the Treasury, the Department of Energy, and "the intelligence elements of the Army, Navy, Air Force, Marine Corps . . . and other elements of any other department or agency as may be designated by the President."

> *Under the Bush administration, we have lost a great deal of personal freedom, and most people are not even aware of it.*

Until and unless the Supreme Court overturns HIPAA's privacy provision [which the Court refused to do in November 2003], the new law will allow law enforcement and national security agencies to ask medical providers (including psychiatrists) for electronic or paper records. If they decline to turn them over, citing the Hippocratic oath as an excuse, officials can serve the providers with "administrative subpoenas," compelling them to hand over the records or face a jail sentence.

Under HIPAA, an administrative subpoena may be served orally.

In 2001, United States attorneys' offices issued 2,102 administrative subpoenas for the FBI "to obtain [medical] records in major U.S. cities from various entities, such as hospitals, nursing homes and individual practitioners," according to a recent U.S. Department of Justice report to Congress. Unlike much evidence uncovered by search warrants, court orders, and grand jury subpoenas, the information gathered through administrative subpoena can be widely circulated among government agencies.

For example, under HIPAA, the bulk of a mental health patient's file might be obtained by the FBI, and then be turned over to the CIA—which might decide to pass it on to the White House.

Loss of Personal Freedom

Given the known activities of [former FBI director] J. Edgar Hoover and [former president] Richard Nixon, one does not necessarily need a conspiratorial mind to imagine possible government misuse of personal information obtained via a HIPAA administrative subpoena. What if a Democrat from a small fly-over state who was rumored to be a womanizer happened to be running for president, and the FBI happened to find out that he'd contracted syphilis during a misspent youth? What if you are a vocal critic of the district attorney, and he lets you know that he knows you are addicted to pain medicine? What if you develop a heart murmur and, suddenly, the promotion you thought was in the bag goes to someone else?

"Under the [George W.] Bush administration, we have lost a great deal of personal freedom, and most people are not even aware of it," says Robert Moffit, a deputy assistant secretary at the Department of Health and Human Services during the [Ronald] Reagan administration who now is director of the Center for Health Policy Studies at the Heritage Foundation in Washington. The right-leaning Heritage Foundation generally objects to government regulation of the health care market, but the Republican-dominated think tank particularly dislikes HIPAA. Several years ago, it joined forces with its natural-born enemy, the American Civil Liberties Union [ACLU], to lobby against the regulations. Both organizations claim that the new rules undermine patient confidentiality and violate the Fourth Amendment by allowing warrantless searches.

Ann Brick, an ACLU staff attorney based in San Francisco, is concerned that national security agencies will use HIPAA and the Patriot Act to search combined medical and consumer databases for particular identifiers, such as "Arab AND diabetes AND airplane mechanic." It goes without saying that the search could be changed to have political parameters, "Democrat AND bipolar," for example.

Actually, HIPAA is more law enforcement friendly in regard to medical records than the oft-criticized Patriot Act, which, at least, requires a judge to sign a court order every time that the FBI or its national security cousins want to search an HMO database, or take a peek at your gynecology file. Unlike the Patriot Act's limited due-process provisions, HIPAA's criteria for issuing subpoenas do not even require judicial review; law enforcers simply have to assert that a medical record or database is "relevant" to an investigation. And HIPAA is slated to outlive the medical-records portion of the Patriot Act, designed to "sunset" in 2005 unless Congress gives it a second life.

> *Police can search medical records without ever having to step before a judge to demonstrate the reasonableness of their request.*

Ohio State University law professor Peter Swire was the White House coordinator for medical privacy rules in the [Bill] Clinton years, and he played an instrumental role in the writing of the HIPAA Privacy Rule. Swire says that, under HIPAA, medical records are not protected by the Fourth Amendment's probable-cause requirement because the Supreme Court has ruled that a person loses "a reasonable expectation of privacy" when his papers (or records) are not in his home. "Once you have voluntarily given over your records to doctor or a bank, they can decide to turn over your records to the police," he says. "It's as if you have given a key to your house to a neighbor."

But Daniel Solove, an associate professor at Seton Hall Law School in New Jersey who has written extensively in national legal journals about Fourth Amendment protections of electronic records, says it is unreasonable to exclude medical records from constitutional protection against unwarranted government search or seizure. "That HIPAA allows law enforcement to take action on a mere administrative subpoena is unconstitutional," Solove says. "For centuries, it has been reasonable for people to expect their doctors to keep their intimate confidences under the Hippocratic oath and the common law."

Changing Fundamental Ethics

In 1971, as the Vietnam War raged, a Defense Department [DOD] analyst named Daniel Ellsberg gave the *New York Times* 47 volumes of secret documents—the Pentagon Papers—showing that American politicians had been systematically lying to the public about events in Vietnam for decades. President Richard Nixon responded by authorizing his aides to burglarize the office of Ellsberg's psychiatrist, in an attempt to discredit the DOD analyst. The aides eventually went to prison, Nixon resigned in disgrace, and Congress passed the Privacy Act of 1974, which greatly limited the government's ability to acquire or to use personal information without a court order.

HIPAA has effectively unwritten the Privacy Act in regard to medical records, and America's psychiatrists are leading the charge against it. "An ethical physician would decline to release information to anyone without patient consent," says Dr. Paul S. Appelbaum, outgoing president of the American Psychiatric Association.

"The government can issue regulations, but it can't change the fundamental ethics that the medical profession has held for several thousand years. We are concerned by the [HIPAA Privacy Rule] provision that would allow for the release of medical information anytime the police are trying to identify a suspect. This broad exception would allow computerized medical records to be sifted through by police to seek matches for blood or other health traits."

Although the Supreme Court has found that psychiatric records enjoy the privilege of physician-patient confidentiality, HIPAA extends that privilege only to the actual notes in which a mental health professional records "the contents of conversation during a private counseling session," and only if those notes are kept separately, i.e., not sprinkled about in the rest of a patient's file. HIPAA does not recognize the existence of a psychiatrist-patient privilege (which is similar to the lawyer-client privilege) for "medication prescription and monitoring, counseling session start and stop times, the modalities and frequencies of treatment furnished, results of clinical tests and any summary of the following items: diagnosis, functional status, the treatment plan, symptoms, prognosis, and progress to date."

This is a shattering change in the classical protections extended to mental health information, says Appelbaum. "For many years, we could say to the police, the FBI, the Secret Service that we don't release information without patient consent or a court order. Law enforcement learned not to ask for such records."

"HIPAA makes it much more likely that doctors and medical facilities will be approached by police and intelligence agencies, and now we have less ammunition to use in the battle to protect patient confidence. The use of administrative subpoenas is a profound change. Police can search medical records without ever having to step before a judge to demonstrate the reasonableness of their request."

Recently, the American Psychoanalytic Association (a national group of 3,500 psychoanalysts not to be conflated with the larger American Psychiatric Association) joined with the Congress of California Seniors, a nonprofit interest group based in Sacramento, in a lawsuit against the federal government. The lawsuit says that HIPAA destroys constitutional protections against governmental abuse of its police powers while it undermines public trust in the integrity of the physician-patient relationship.

Bill Powers of the Congress of California Seniors says that his group's 600,000 retirees are afraid that improper disclosures of their medical and psychiatric records will negatively affect their chances to get jobs, health insurance, and loans. "Under the guise of protecting our privacy rights," says Powers, "the Bush administration is imposing on our rights."

6

Federal Law Protects Medical Privacy

Richard Campanelli

Richard Campanelli is the director of the Office for Civil Rights at the U.S. Department of Health and Human Services.

In 2003 Congress passed the Health Insurance Portability and Accountability Act (HIPAA), which has provisions to protect the privacy of patients' medical records and other health information. Even before the act was signed into law, the Office for Civil Rights (OCR) within the Department of Health and Human Services was working to protect patient privacy. The OCR collected thousands of comments concerning privacy rights from consumers, doctors, and other medical professionals. They took these comments into account when developing HIPAA's rigorous Privacy Rule provision, the first national standard ever passed into law for protecting medical privacy. While this complex government program may not be perfect, the OCR is committed to letting individuals choose how their personal medical records are used so that their privacy is assured.

C ongress enacted HIPAA [Health Insurance Portability and Accountability Act] in 1996, among other things, to improve the efficiency and effectiveness of the health care system, through "administrative simplification" provisions that created a process for the establishment of standards and requirements for the electronic transmission of certain health information. At the same time, Congress recognized that administrative simplification must be accompanied by protections for the privacy

Richard Campanelli, statement before the U.S. Senate Special Committee on Aging, Washington, DC, September 23, 2003.

and confidentiality of personal health information, since, as a consequence of more efficient transmission of health information, private health information also would become more readily accessible. Therefore, in enacting HIPAA Congress directed that standards be developed to protect the security and privacy of health information, and established civil and criminal penalties for various violations of those standards. Pursuant to Congress' mandate, HHS [Department of Health and Human Services] issued a proposed Privacy Rule in November 1999, received over 50,000 public comments, and published a final Privacy Rule in December of 2000. Because of continuing concern over aspects of the Rule, in February 2001, HHS announced that it would reopen the Rule for comments, and, after receiving thousands of comments, in April 2001 it proposed to issue recommended modifications to avoid the unintended consequences of the Privacy Rule and improve its workability. Those proposed modifications were published in April 2002, and received some 11,000 additional comments. Finally, just over a year ago, on August 14, 2002, HHS finalized those modifications to improve workability while maintaining strong privacy protections. As covered entities have known since the Rule took effect, most covered entities were required to comply with the Privacy Rule as of April 14, 2003, with small health plans having an additional year to comply.

> *Congress directed that standards be developed to protect the security and privacy of health information, and established civil and criminal penalties for various violations of those standards.*

The Privacy Rule establishes the Nation's first-ever comprehensive standards for protecting the privacy of Americans' personal health records. As of April 14, 2003, patients have sweeping federal protections over the privacy of their medical records, rights to access and to correct errors in their medical records, rights to control how their protected health information is used and disclosed, and a clear avenue of recourse if the rights afforded by the Privacy Rule are violated. . . .

One area of the Privacy Rule that was modified on August

14, which had been the subject of much public response during the comment period, was the requirement to obtain written consents from patients to use or disclose their protected health information to treat them, obtain payment, or carry out day-to-day operations. Requiring consent in these contexts would have been unnecessarily burdensome on patients and providers, and interfered with timely access to quality care, without improving privacy. It would have meant, for instance, that a doctor would have needed a patient to sign a privacy consent before he could use health information to treat that patient; that a specialist contacted by the patient's doctor would have needed to obtain the patient's consent to read treatment information; and that a pharmacist would have needed the patient's consent to fill a prescription written by the provider.

> **// The Privacy Rule establishes the Nation's first-ever comprehensive standards for protecting the privacy of Americans' personal health records. //**

The Privacy Rule modifications removed the requirement that providers must obtain prior consent to use or disclose a patient's health information for treatment, payment or health care operations purposes. While obtaining such consent is optional, this change assured that providers would have ready access to health information about their patients, and could readily share that information for treatment, for payment, and for health care operations so that timely access to quality health care would not be unduly impeded. At the same time, we strengthened the notice requirement by requiring direct treatment providers to make a good faith effort to obtain the patient's written acknowledgment that they received the notice. This ensures that a patient has the opportunity to consider the provider's privacy practices, both to be better informed of how their information may or may not be disclosed, and to be informed of their rights—which had been a primary goal of the consent requirement. Notably, the Privacy Rule retained the protections that give patients the right to decide whether to authorize uses or disclosures of their information for marketing purposes, or to employers. . . .

The Privacy Rule recognizes that communications necessary for quick, effective and high quality health care might unavoidably lead to overheard communications. Thus, a physician may discuss a patient's condition or treatment regimen in the patient's semi-private room, and a pharmacist may discuss a prescription with a patient over the pharmacy counter, provided that reasonable precautions (such as lowered voices and/or talking apart from others) are employed.

Both of these examples demonstrate how the Privacy Rule, as modified, both protects patient information, but avoids imposing unnecessary impediments to quality health care.

Explaining Consumer Rights

Since April 14, 2003 there has been widespread compliance by health plans, health care clearinghouses, and those providers covered by the Privacy Rule ("Covered Entities"). For example, physicians, hospitals, clinics, pharmacies, health insurance carriers, employer group health plans and others have distributed Notices, required by the Privacy Rule, that tell consumers about how their health information can and cannot be used and disclosed, and their rights, including:

• the right to inspect and obtain a copy of the individual's protected health information;

• the right to amend or correct protected health information;

• the right to request restrictions on certain uses and disclosures of protected health information;

• the right to receive protected health information through confidential communications;

• the right to receive an accounting of certain disclosures of their protected health information;

• the right to receive a copy of the Notice of Privacy Practices; and

• the right to complain to a covered entity or to OCR [the Office of Civil Rights] if an individual believes a covered entity has breached the Privacy Rule.

Given the extensive scope of the protections established in the Privacy Rule, implementation has gone smoothly, without the disruption of the health care system that had been predicted in some quarters. . . .

As I will explain OCR has contributed to reducing confusion and eliminating misconceptions that have been reported in these first months of compliance. In many of these areas, confusion appears to have arisen not because of problems with the Privacy Rule itself, but rather due to misconceptions about it. In addition, it appears that providers and other covered entities are also serving to educate their fellow covered entities where overly restrictive practices were initially being adopted and, incorrectly, blamed on the Privacy Rule.

For example, we have heard reports that some covered entities are reluctant to share health information with other providers, for the purpose of treating their patients, claiming that the Privacy Rule requires that patients execute written consents for these disclosures to occur. Providers who claim that this practice is mandated by the Privacy Rule are incorrect, and apparently are unaware that the Rule was modified specifically to permit treatment disclosures among providers without the need for patient consent. In fact, the Privacy Rule allows doctors, nurses, hospitals, technicians, and other covered health care providers to use or disclose patient health information, including X-rays, laboratory and pathology reports, diagnoses, and other medical information for treatment purposes, without the patient's authorization. This includes sharing a patient's health information to consult with other providers, to treat a different patient, or to refer the patient to other providers.

> *A doctor . . . can disclose any information that is directly relevant to the family member or friend's involvement with the patient's care, or payment related to the individual's care.*

Similarly, we have seen reports and heard from consumers . . . that providers cannot share information with family members, loved ones, friends, or others whom are identified by the individual as involved in their care or the payment for their care. Again, rather than foreclosing such communications, the Privacy Rule provides a number of common-sense methods which appropriately permit such disclosures while respecting and protecting an individual's right to control their health information. . . . The Privacy Rule specifically permits covered entities to share information that is directly relevant to the involvement of a spouse, family members, friends, or other persons identified by a patient, in the patient's care or payment for health care. Where the patient is present and has the capacity to make health care decisions, the covered entity may discuss this information with these individuals if the patient agrees or, when given the opportunity, does not object. The covered entity may also share relevant information with these individuals if it can reasonably infer, based on professional judgment, that the patient does not object. For example, if a patient brings a friend to a medical appointment and asks if the friend can come into the treatment room, her doctor can reasonably infer that the patient does not object. Under these circumstances, a doctor or plan can disclose any information that is directly relevant to the family member or friend's involvement with the patient's care, or payment related to the individual's care. . . .

Letting Individuals Choose

We have also heard reports—incorrect, again—that because of the Privacy Rule, hospitals can no longer maintain patient directories so that appropriate information can be provided to family members, loved ones, clergy or other members of the public who call to inquire about patients. Along similar lines, we have seen reports that clergy, in particular, can no longer visit members of their congregations in the hospital, because the Privacy Rule forbids clergy access to any information about hospitalized individuals, or to information about the individual's religious affiliation. Though it does not mandate that hospitals maintain such directories or make such disclosures, the Privacy Rule specifically provides and envisions that the common and helpful practice of maintaining such directories will continue. Consistent with the overall approach of the Rule, it lets individuals choose whether their information should be included in the facility directory, or to opt out. Even where, because of emergency or the individual's incapacity, the patient cannot be given the opportunity to opt out, the Privacy Rule allows the covered entity to determine, based on experience and professional judgment, whether including the information would be in the best interests of the patient. This information—including the patient's name, location in the hospital, and general description of the patient's condition—can be accessed by anyone inquiring about the patient by name.

Clergy similarly can access this information by asking for

patients by name, of course; but the Privacy Rule also allows hospitals to include in the facility directory, and to disclose to members of the clergy, the religious affiliation of patients who have opted to provide it; and members of the clergy can obtain this information without having to inquire about specific patients by name. As with disclosures of information in facility directories to other members of the public, the patient (or those with appropriate authority to act on their behalf) will have the opportunity to decide whether they want their information included in the directory, or to opt out. If they elect to have the information included, then their loved ones, clergy, or others who inquire can have access to this information.

The misconceptions discussed here are among the most common we have heard. It appears that confusion on these issues is dissipating, as covered entities and consumers become more familiar with the Rule's requirements. These problems do not arise because of the Privacy Rule, but rather seem to arise either because providers have elected to take a more restrictive approach than the Privacy Rule requires, or because of a misconception about the requirements of the Privacy Rule. To address this latter concern, OCR has conducted, and is continuing to conduct, an extensive public education effort to produce and disseminate a wide range of guidance about various aspects of the Rule that are of concern to the public and to covered entities. And we are pleased that the information we have disseminated is being well received.

7

The Right to Privacy Is Destroyed by Video Cameras in Public Places

Molly Smithsimon

Molly Smithsimon is a New York City attorney at the Community Service Society and directs an advocacy group for tenants living in federally assisted housing.

Americans are losing their privacy to tens of thousands of video cameras operated by private corporations and government authorities. People are being watched when they shop, drive, attend sporting events, or simply walk down the street. This constant surveillance creates a general uneasiness, restrains private behavior, and inhibits political speech at demonstrations. Those who promote video surveillance claim that society is safer when all citizens are under observation. However, the loss of anonymity violates the right of people to be secure from unreasonable government intrusion into their private lives.

If you liked [the TV show] *Survivor*, just imagine a new reality-based television show that captures New Yorkers in their most intimate public moments. You'd see politicians' daughters buying drugs in Tompkins Square Park, topless tanning in Central Park, and CEOs stumbling out of midtown bars after having a few too many. Why not? In a culture like ours that

Molly Smithsimon, "Private Lives, Public Spaces: The Surveillance State," *Dissent,* Winter 2003. Copyright © 2003 by Dissent Publishing Corporation. Reproduced by permission.

thrives on voyeuristic thrills, the show would no doubt be a hit. Viewers in the United Kingdom were treated to a compilation of "juicy bits" from government closed circuit television (CCTV) cameras when Barrie Goulding launched *Caught in the Act*. The program featured the sexual and other intimate activities of innocent people as well as lawbreakers. Great Britain, the spawning ground of reality television, has 1.5 million television cameras monitoring the public, more than any other nation, but the United States is rapidly catching up.

Thousands of cameras, both publicly and privately owned, dot city streets and parks. Once someone has gone out in public, courts have refused to recognize any expectation of privacy from being watched on camera, either by private (in tort law) or government (under the Fourth Amendment) actors. But people are, by and large, unaware that they are being watched. Nor do they know or control what their images are being used for. The problem is compounded by the potential use of facial recognition technology to compare the faces of people who simply step into public places with the database images of suspects and convicted criminals, an action that in other forms would require probable cause. Law enforcement's track record of disproportionately targeting racial and ethnic minorities, combined with the high rate of false positive matches, makes it likely that innocent people will be arrested without any independent justification.

Electronic surveillance has sent a detectable chill through our public spaces. The first clause of the Fourth Amendment declares, "The right of the people to be secure in their persons, houses, papers and effects, against unreasonable searches and seizures shall not be violated." A faithful reading allows a reasonable expectation of freedom from searching scrutiny of one's person, papers and effects wherever one is, including outside on public streets and in parks. No case has squarely faced this issue, and the current Supreme Court would likely find that electronic monitoring of public areas is not a search subject to Fourth Amendment scrutiny. Chief Justice William Rehnquist has made clear his views that law enforcement interests will generally trump any limited right to privacy while out in public. However, if the Court adopted a more honest test, it would recognize the distinction between what is actually in plain view (and hence reasonable to observe) and what is capable of being seen if technology is trained on the public in ways it doesn't and shouldn't expect.

No unreasonable search occurs when a beat police officer glances around or even stops to survey passersby. But when law enforcement films the public engaging in all the activities of mundane existence, the government crosses the line. Even more invasive is taping video footage, using nightscopes, and using biometric technology to analyze the faces or carriage of presumptively innocent citizens to find matches with criminal suspects. Biometric technology, which has been piloted in Tampa, Florida; in airports in Boston, Providence, San Francisco, and Fresno; and at checkpoints at the U.S.-Mexico border, may appear to be a "perfect search" because it is supposed to single out only known offenders. But in reality, the rate of error vastly exceeds accurate matches.

Electronic Eyes

As part of the 1998 New York Civil Liberties Union Surveillance Camera Project, volunteers walked every block in Manhattan and found 2,397 publicly and privately controlled cameras trained on public spaces. The thickest concentrations are in midtown, the financial district in lower Manhattan parks, and around housing projects. In one eight-block radius alone, volunteers noted three hundred cameras. But there are likely many thousands more because of the routine security practice of buttressing visible cameras with concealed ones "so everything's covered and it doesn't look like a fortress," a consultant told the *Village Voice*. Public cameras are typically mounted on traffic and streetlight poles, public buildings and trees and installed in buses, on subway platforms, and inside subway cars. The full extent of saturation isn't known, because police officials refuse to divulge their locations, claiming that it would undermine law enforcement's effectiveness, and besides, the majority of cameras are nongovernmental, owned by countless private companies.

Bill Brown, founder of the privacy watchdog group The Surveillance Camera Players, gives walking tours of New York City surveillance camera locations. He estimates there are about six thousand cameras in Manhattan. He noted some of the questions, constitutional and commercial, raised by an unmarked camera. "In addition to watching the front door, it's also pointing out into public space and recording information about the passersby: Who are they with? What are they wearing? What are they smoking? Are they drinking Coca-Cola or Pepsi?"

Penetrating Stares

A number of factors make an electronic eye inherently more in-trusive than direct observation by a human being. Law profes-sor and legal columnist Sherry Colb notes that you can't stare back to discourage the privacy incursion. Nor can you choose to move away from the area under surveillance if you don't know where it is. People behave differently when they think they are alone. A Tampa police-camera operator, Raymond Green, told the St. *Petersburg Times:* "Some things are really funny, like the way people dance when they think no one's looking." On the other hand, even if people are aware of the cameras, this does not alleviate the problems. As Colb signals, awareness that we are being watched by surveillance cameras can put us in a "constant state of apprehension and self-consciousness whenever we are out in public." Sociologist Steven Flusty aptly calls this monitored public space "jittery space." Rather than promoting the ideals of a democratic soci-ety, it creates a police state environment that chills the exercise of First Amendment rights and further polarizes race relations.

Police officers have long singled out African-Americans and other people of color for mistreatment. Camera operators may be even more likely to target members of stigmatized social groups for monitoring when the public can't see them. From a control room it's easier to single one person out, and it's less noticeable. Colb identifies targeting as a secondary, but impor-tant, privacy harm. When a person is singled out by police with no legitimate basis, he or she is left asking, "What made them think I'm a criminal?"

Criminologists Clive Norris and Gary Armstrong answer that question in their study of CCTV monitoring in Great Britain. In the absence of concrete guidance on whom to monitor, "CCTV operators selectively target those social groups they believe most likely to be deviant." The most over-represented characteristics of those scrutinized were maleness, youth, and blackness. Oper-ators also focused on anyone running or loitering, even though this rarely led to finding criminal conduct (of course, disorderly conduct also attracted the operator's attention); anyone who ap-peared to be spatially or temporally out of place—the most ob-vious being drunks, beggars, the homeless and street vendors; people whose clothing style signaled they were trouble-makers; people who challenged the authority of the camera to watch them; and people who seemed to be trying to conceal their iden-tity. Norris and Armstrong found that nearly four out of ten people were monitored for "no obvious reason."

Cameras do not merely serve the purpose of an automated beat cop, contrary to courts' assumptions. They are more like super cops. Video feeds can be linked to a nationwide or international database to scan for matches with criminal suspects (though thus far such efforts have faltered because facial recognition software is so imperfect). Images can be enhanced far beyond the visual capabilities of a human being. The cameras can view faces a hundred yards away, see in the dark with infrared technology, and zoom in to read a letter someone is holding, which police couldn't do without probable cause. Furthermore, they can be placed in a position where a person couldn't be, such as high up on a wall.

> *Cameras do not merely serve the purpose of an automated beat cop, contrary to courts' assumptions. They are more like super cops.*

The potential for abuse is considerable: the technology could easily be used for sexual voyeurism, racial profiling, or to harass gays, lesbians, and transgendered people. Unlike the eye simply catching a fleeting glance of an embarrassing moment, the camera makes it permanent and possible to disseminate widely. The *Detroit Free Press*, found that Detroit officers used the video database of the Law Enforcement Information Network to help themselves or their friends stalk women, threaten motorists after road rage incidents involving the police as drivers, and intimidate supporters of political rivals.

In weighing the intrusiveness of cameras, courts suggest comparing the privacy incursion against law enforcement needs; we also need further comparison with the proportion of positive outcomes. Of all the people subjected to electronic lineups in stadium scans at the Superbowl, the system succeeded only in flagging some petty criminals, such as ticket scalpers, not the menaces to society, such as terrorists and violent criminals, that officials claimed to be targeting with the searches. In Tampa, an experiment with Face-IT, a face recognition application, never correctly identified a single face in its database of suspects and didn't result in a single arrest, but had many false positives.

Although cameras are billed as necessary to prevent serious crimes, they are used to raise revenue and catch relatively minor offenders. New York City, San Diego, and Washington, D.C., use cameras at bus stops and intersections to ticket illegally parked vehicles and catch speeders and red-light runners. After data were released in San Diego, the court threw out hundreds of traffic tickets. The data showed that accidents at monitored intersections actually increased. The city's vendor company (Lockheed Martin IMS) had shortened the yellow-light time to capture more offenders. In Great Britain, the Environment Agency installed a tiny camera in a discarded Coke can to catch people in the criminal act of dumping trash, at a cost of 3,500 pounds (or about $5,000). . . .

Chilling Effects

Private and police cameras essentially have the same function: to protect private property. And both have a similar effect of making video-monitored space feel controlled, not free and public. But it would feel very different if we knew that Big Brother was watching—if all the cameras were linked and their control centralized in law enforcement command centers. Feelings of paranoia would be justified because private viewers are much less likely to be upset by behavior that police may find egregious. For example, on the highway there is a distinction between driving so badly that people around you will use their cell phones to call the police, and driving well enough to satisfy the police officer cruising along behind you.

Contemporary sociologists argue that surveillance has the potential to control the population by keeping social groups apart. In their separate case studies of Los Angeles, urban sociologists Steven Flusty and Mike Davis discuss how heightened surveillance has undermined the potential for interaction between individuals and different social groups, and essentially eviscerated democratic public space. Public streets, parks, and plazas have traditionally provided an arena to "synthesize new cultures, alternative ways of living and popular forces occasionally strong enough to upset entrenched status quos," notes Flusty. Access to city spaces should be guaranteed by virtue of citizenship, but it is increasingly becoming a privilege conferred by status. Surveillance implies that users are not to be trusted; "flawed consumers and other undesirables" pick up on the message that the space is monitored and controlled by the corporations that foot the bill for the security towers and cameras at Los Angeles malls. In *City of Quartz*, Mike Davis described how the Los Angeles Police Department "relentlessly" restricts uses of public spaces and the free movement and association of youths by enforcing juvenile curfews, barricading boulevards, and sealing off entire neighborhoods and public housing projects. Available public spaces are increasingly circumscribed as the wealthy elite of Los Angeles construct gated residential communities to exclude the marginalized and ghettoized underclass and use CCTV to police the boundaries and ensure prompt responses to incursions. Flusty underscores the dystopian potential of a fortress city coupled with maximum surveillance:

> Los Angeles is undergoing the intervention and installation, component by component, of a physical infrastructure engendering electronically linked islands of privilege embedded in a police state matrix. If left unchecked, this trend may be linearly extrapolated into a worst case composite of hard boundaries, checkpoints and omnipresent surveillance. Los Angeles will become a city consisting of numerous fortified cores of private space, each augmented by more permeable outer perimeters of contorted paths, lights, motion detectors, and video cameras projecting in the public realm of the sidewalk and the street. The public streets will become little more than the interstitial space to these fortified private cores.

Police and the military often use surveillance to intimidate protestors. Recent examples include mass demonstrations against the joint World Bank and International Monetary Fund meeting in April 2000, the mainstream Million Family March in October 2000, and protests against George W. Bush's inauguration in January 2001. According to social psychologists, a participant's self-image can be affected by taping, because being a subject of surveillance is unconsciously associated with criminality. The message is clear: "hang with dissenters, and you'll end up in a police video," [reporter Mark] Boal observes. . . .

Voyeurism

Video surveillance and facial recognition are easy to sell to a public more paranoid than ever before about terrorists, murderers, rapists, child molesters, cop killers, robbers, and prison escapees in our midst. What could be less objectionable than catching terrorists? Each intrusion is introduced as being a tool against the pariah group or issue: drug testing, once just for high security jobs, is now being implemented against secretaries at your local Board of Education and students who participate in extracurricular activities; EZ Pass [automated toll collection] was introduced to alleviate traffic congestion, and is now used to track speeding remotely and issue tickets; it could be used in the future to trace people's whereabouts. After the technology has been implemented with one justification, over little public objection, we can be sure that it will be used for a much wider range of everyday activities and against many more people. Sociologist Gary Marx warns, "Once the new surveillance systems become institutionalized and taken for granted in a democratic society," they can be "used against those with the 'wrong' political beliefs; against racial, ethnic, or religious minorities; and against those with lifestyles that offend the majority."

Contrary to the assumptions of privacy jurisprudence, reasonable people do not intend to waive all rights to privacy when they appear in public. Reasonable people trust that their privacy will be more respected than the law recognizes. If we use a contextual approach to determining the contours of Fourth Amendment privacy in public spaces, we see that constant video surveillance is clearly inappropriate and a violation of the government's mandate to leave people free from unreasonable searches and seizures. Fundamental values of autonomy and freedom of association are crucial to the vitality of a democratic society. And public privacy is essential to guarantee equal access to the benefits of privacy. If it is confined to private spaces, it becomes available only to the affluent. Under this regime, of course, homeless people, who have committed no crime, have no defensible right to privacy. There is a whole range of socially productive interactions that can only happen outside—in particular, anything involving people we don't already know, or anything unplanned, unexpected, or kept secret from the people we live with. Our legal regime should protect our trust and the values that underlie it, not undermine it with unchecked spying.

8

Video Cameras Help Police While Protecting the Public

William D. Eggers and Eve Tushnet

William D. Eggers is a senior fellow and Eve Tushnet a research associate at the Manhattan Institute, a conservative think tank that provides policy statements on taxes, welfare, crime, race relations, and other urban issues.

Video surveillance provides a sense of security. For example, women walking through a deserted parking garage may appreciate knowing that security guards are using cameras to keep them safe. New technology is allowing police to link the cameras to computers that can instantly recognize criminals and terrorists. Critics fear this crime-fighting tool will be misused by authorities who might use the cameras to intimidate certain groups such as political protesters. However, as long as proper safeguards are in place to protect innocent citizens from overzealous video spies, these cameras should be seen as a welcome part of modern life.

Government cameras are watching you—at red lights across America, . . . And it's not going to stop. Already, in London's Liverpool Street Station, they're testing robot cameras that will signal a cop if we display suspicious behavior. Former House Majority Leader Dick Armey (R-Texas) asks: "Do we really want a society where one cannot walk down the street without Big Brother tracking our every move?"

William D. Eggers and Eve Tushnet, "Big Brother's Eyes," *New York Post*, May 2, 2002. Copyright © 2002 by the *New York Post*. Reproduced by permission.

Well, no. But the future need not be so grim. We've been living with cameras for years now—but few of us worry about cameras at the 7-11 or the ATM. We can live with more of them if we act now to safeguard privacy against potential governmental abuses.

Many civil libertarians insist that the only way to protect privacy is through prohibition: Tear down the cameras. Ban government from using face-recognition and other biometric technologies.

Sounds good, but it won't work. For one thing, the spycams are already here. Fully 80 percent of America's 19,000 police departments are already using them, according to the International Association of Chiefs of Police. And Congress is highly unlikely to pass a law forcing every city in the country to take down their cameras.

What's more, the "ban everything" approach ignores the technologies' plain benefits. Any woman who's had to walk through a deserted parking garage to her car knows why many people might welcome cameras.

Cameras Do the Watching

With many advances still ahead, computer-linked surveillance cameras can already identify crimes as they occur, reduce false arrests and convictions and provide much better evidence than notoriously unreliable witness testimony. Linked to biometric databases [that can store people's digitized facial features], the cameras can help prevent fraud, find a lost child and keep terrorists out of airports and pedophiles out of schools.

The cameras aren't going away. Fortunately, with some care we can reap the benefits of these technologies without worrying about waking up in [a police state]. . . .

Let machines do the watching: A basic objection to the cameras is their creepiness. Many women may like the feeling of extra security the cameras provide, but others will wonder whether the invisible person controlling the camera is a bored man who's zooming in on her chest. Reducing human involvement and maximizing that of machines can help prevent this problem, as well as easing the fear that the cameras might target certain groups like gay couples, political protestors and swarthy-looking men.

Once the technology is made more accurate, cameras equipped with face-recognition technology could do the bulk of the "watching," alerting humans only when they find a positive face match that needs verification. In the case of London's "robot cameras" and other behavioral-recognition technology, the cameras will be programmed to set off an alert when they detect suspicious movements such as fighting, weapon use or going from vehicle to vehicle at a parking garage (often a sign that a car thief is scoping out targets).

Limit how long the information is kept: Law-enforcement agencies will want to keep the information forever, but the threats to liberty from giving the government the ability to compile retrospective dossiers on any citizen outweigh the security advantages. With the exception of material needed for criminal investigations, the tapes should be destroyed within a reasonable time period.

Watch the watchers: Many police departments install cameras on squad cars to knock down false police brutality charges, but the cameras also record real uses of excessive force. Public defender Don Landis Jr. represented one arrestee whose case was dismissed after the videotape of his arrest proved that the arresting officer had lied. Landis noted, "The cameras bring accountability."

Video cameras are also used by agencies to videotape interrogations. In Charlottesville, Va., a detective was charged with assault after an interrogation camera caught him beating a suspect.

Inform the public: During the 1989 Tiananmen Square demonstrations, student protestors were identified with surveillance cameras that purportedly had been installed to monitor traffic, but in reality were being used to secretly keep tabs on how many times Chinese met with foreigners.

To prevent such a thing from ever happening in America, surveillance technology should be used openly, and as much information as possible must be given to the public regarding where it is in use, the reasons for its use and what safeguards exist to prevent abuses. There should also be sanctions—legally and in the court of public opinion—for politicians, cops or anyone else who breaks these rules.

In the end, of course, all of our liberties depend upon a vigilant culture that will revile anyone who misuses a video database to draw up anything like an "electronic enemies list." If we don't care about police or government abuses, we'll get them no matter what technology we use; if we do watch the watchers, no camera will protect an abuser from the press and the populace.

9

Facial Recognition Technology Represents a Threat to Privacy

Daniel J. Melinger

Daniel J. Melinger is the cofounder of the Kamida software company.

Within the next decade, governments, employers, and marketers will probably be able to identify people using facial recognition technology or other forms of biometrics. The U.S. government is already testing facial recognition technology for many uses, including protection against terrorists and criminals. The facial characteristics of most people could be stored in huge government databases used to track and locate suspects. Biometrics will not only be used to search for criminals but will also be employed by businesses to monitor workers and even the buying habits and emotions of shoppers in a mall. Although biometrics can serve good purposes, it also poses a threat to privacy because those using the technology will be able to get information about people's locations and habits. Some organizations, such as the American Civil Liberties Union, therefore oppose the use of facial recognition technology.

[The following fictional scenario could be reality within the next decade:] Jennifer had visited a friend who lives in Medford, Massachusetts, a small suburb of Boston, for the weekend. But it was Sunday morning and time for her to drive back home to Philadelphia. After driving a few blocks from her

Daniel J. Melinger, "Facial Recognition Technology, Future of the Infrastructure," http://fargo.itp.tsoa.nyu.edu, 2002. Copyright © 2002 by Daniel J. Melinger. Reproduced by permission.

friend's house, Jennifer pulls onto the main road in the suburb, a state-managed route replete with strip malls and chain restaurants. At the traffic light, before Jennifer turns onto the Massachusetts state route, a camera operated by a computer server in the state office of Homeland Security gets a glimpse of her through her [windshield]. The camera sends a video stream to the server, which digitally reorients Jennifer's face, calculates her faceprint, and then begins to search for a match in the databases to which it has access. Within a small fraction of a second, the server's logic realizes that the person in the car doesn't match any of the entries for the 55,000 residents of the municipality or the 1.5 million residents of Middlesex county. Then it checks her against the remainder of the Massachusetts records—still no match. It must access the federal database, a copy of which is stored at the state office. A few seconds after catching her on camera, it finds that Jennifer is a resident of Philadelphia.

If needed, the server could correlate this information with a multitude of personal data, including her travel history, federal tax information, criminal record, and public library records. However, Jennifer's movements and habits haven't raised any major flags before. The server's fuzzy logic assumes she's probably just traveling out of town on business or pleasure. Her national account's warning level will be raised a notch to indicate that she should be more closely watched for the next fifteen hours, but this isn't enough to warrant intervention. On the other hand, if she took State Route 3 south along the coast and got out of her car near Pilgrim nuclear power plant in Plymouth, her warning level would get a little hotter.

A Way to Identify People

Facial recognition technology is hardware and software that allows computers to identify people by their faces. It is a subset of biometrics, other examples of which include fingerprint scans, retinal scans, and voice identification. While humans have an innate ability to easily recognize the faces of other humans, even within large crowds and when factors such as emotion, facial hair, and age change the faces' appearance, it has proven difficult to teach computers to perform this task. However, over the past decades, much effort has been put toward making computers better at facial recognition. Computers have been trained to identify people based on their faceprint, a combination of fourteen to twenty-two facial attributes, such as the distance between the eyes, the width of the nose, the depth of the eye sockets, and properties of the cheekbones, jaw line, and chin. The technology is beginning to become a viable way to identify people in various scenarios such as law enforcement, security surveillance, eliminating voter fraud, bank transaction identity verification, and computer security.

While some activist organizations assert that facial recognition technology is inaccurate and ineffective and will remain so for the foreseeable future, most biometrics experts agree that the technology already works to a large degree and will quickly become more effective. As privacy advocacy organizations, civil liberty organizations, and some private individuals lobby to remove facial recognition technology from mainstream use, government institutions, private companies, and private security firms continue to push for its use. Recently, attitudes in the US have caused a push for greater security at the expense of privacy. These attitudes have been influenced greatly by the events of September 11, 2001, and the increased fears of terrorism that followed.

Government and Private Industry

In the US, various government groups are testing facial recognition technology, pushing for the furthering of its development, and putting it to use. In the US government, the Biometrics Management Office of the Department of Defense, with its Biometrics Fusion Center, is overseeing a number of initiatives with the purpose of testing and researching facial recognition technology. . . . The Office was established in 2000 to be a proponent for biometrics in the D.O.D [Department of Defense]. Though not stated in its official mission, the Office is also a key facilitator of the biometrics industry, bringing industry, academic, and government stakeholders together. The Department of Defense Counterdrug Technology Department Program Office also sponsored the Face Recognition Technology (FERET) program at the National Institute of Standards and Technology. This program was established to sponsor research, to create a database of facial images, and to evaluate the accuracy of technologies from various vendors.

Facial recognition technology is being developed by hundreds of different companies. Identix uses technology developed by Visionics, a company that Identix merged with in 2002. Identix bills their facial recognition technology, dubbed FaceIt

ARGUS, as revolutionizing closed-circuit television security systems and as "plug-and-play" [meaning users will be able to operate the system quickly and easily]. Their product literature emphasizes ease of installation, effectiveness, and compatibility with existing security systems. Another company, Viisage markets technology originally developed at the Massachusetts Institute of Technology. Viisage breaks their products down into different sectors, ranging from identity authorization in the use of personal computers to the identity of "potential threats to public safety." After September 11, 2001, when equities markets experienced a broad slump, the stock prices of both Visionics and Viisage rose, showing investors' confidence in facial recognition technology as a way to combat terrorism.

In addition to everyday use, facial recognition technology has been utilized in several well-publicized events. In 2001, all people entering a Tampa, Florida, stadium to attend the Superbowl had their faces scanned in a test of Viisage's product. This resulted in a flurry of backlash against facial recognition technology as an invasion of privacy. In a trial seen as more positive and successful, Visionics' facial recognition technology was used in the Mexican presidential elections of 2000 to help minimize voter fraud through multiple registrations. Both Viisage and Visionics' products are currently being tested at Boston's Logan Airport to allow frequent fliers to Britain to enjoy a smoother security check process before flying.

Along with the many deployments and tests of facial recognition technology, some organizations are fighting its use. The American Civil Liberties Union [ACLU] opposes the use of facial recognition technology. The ACLU claims that the technology represents an invasion of privacy and is ineffective and that it should not be used for these reasons. The Electronic Privacy Information Center seems to be carefully watching the technology, and its impacts on privacy.

How the Technology Will Be Used

To assist in evaluating how the technology will be used in 2010, I have identified four major categories of uses: (1) government surveillance, (2) private security surveillance, (3), marketing support, and (4) identity verification.

Government surveillance: Over the coming years, the US government and governments around the world will employ more facial recognition technology to watch their citizens and to look for outsiders. This will make these countries safer places to live but will also hinder personal liberties and privacy. Citizens, on the whole will reluctantly accept the need for these technologies as the new reality.

Private security surveillance: Private companies will employ the technology to watch their workers and to protect their assets and real estate. This will help companies to stay competitive, but will affect the privacy of individuals watched. It will also cause worker backlash in some instances as workers show that they are not always comfortable working in watched environments.

Marketing support: As the technologies get better, consumer-directed companies will use facial recognition technology in retail settings and for marketing in general. Computers will begin to track buyers' habits and emotions. Armed with this information, marketers will be able to tailor offerings to consumers and to track consumer behavior. This will lead toward increased ability to compete in the companies that utilize the technology and a feeling of loss of privacy for consumers.

Identity verification: Facial recognition technology will be used more and more to verify the identity of people. Whether it is to gain access to an office building, to log into a computer, or to register to vote, facial recognition technology will allow those using the technology to be more assured of whom they are working with. While the direct effects of these uses are no doubt positive, the secondary effect is that those using the technology will have increased information about where people are and about their habits.

It seems inevitable that facial recognition technology will be developed to the point where it is significantly successful. It is questionable as to whether the technology will be advanced enough to identify individuals in large moving crowds by 2010, but nevertheless, it will probably be a viable technology for many uses by this date. It is also quite likely that facial recognition will become the biometrics technology of choice as software and hardware gets better. Currently, other processes, such as retinal scans are commonly used, but the advantages of facial recognition, such as the ability to scan from a distance, will cause more people to adopt it in the future.

10

Physical Characteristic Recognition Technology Can Be Used to Preserve Privacy Rights

Solveig Singleton

Solveig Singleton is a lawyer and senior analyst with the Competitive Enterprise Institute's Project on Technology and Innovation. She specializes in the analysis of privacy, electronic commerce, and telecommunications.

Americans are accustomed to presenting driver's licenses or other forms of identification when conducting business transactions or entering secured areas such as airports. Most forms of ID, however, are easily counterfeited, and terrorists and criminals have easy access to these fraudulent documents. This problem is eliminated by biometric technology that creates digital pictures of facial features, fingerprints, and other unique physical characteristics. While civil libertarians fear a world where every person's digital identifiers are in the hands of authorities, biometrics can play an important part in the fight against crime and terrorism. Biometrics can also help protect privacy. For example, access to personal computers or financial records could be restricted only to those who have the proper digital identifiers. Like any other system of identification, biometrics could be used to violate privacy rights. It is not the technology, however, that needs oversight, but the government departments that use it.

Solveig Singleton, "Authoritarianism Is Not a Gadget, It's a State of Mind," *Insight on the News*, February 25, 2002. Copyright © 2002 by News World Communications, Inc. All rights reserved. Reproduced by permission.

The two dark-skinned young men, unshaven and heavily muscled, looked ominously foreign. No doubt more than one airline passenger breathed deeper in relief when security guards at the Roanoke, Va., airport pulled the men out of line to search their luggage and pat them down—once in the ticket line, again at the security gate and a third time before they boarded the plane. Three "random" searches to take a 20-minute flight.

Facial-recognition technology tied to a database of suspected terrorists, though, would have left the young men alone. My black-haired fiancé and his brother are no threat. Their frightening musculature is cheerfully employed shifting furniture for their mom; their closest approach to battle is the world of online computer games. Yet the human element in our security forces instinctively will bristle at their approach until the United States is attacked by blond, blue-eyed Nordic terrorists, activists for reindeer rights or some myth of Aryan superiority.

> **// As the cost of this technology comes down and its accuracy is improved, widespread deployment in the private sector is almost a given. //**

Biometrics are getting a bad rap. Fingerprinting bears the stigma of its association with police procedure. DNA databases bring to mind horrific theories of genetic or racial purity. Facial-recognition cameras call up images of George Orwell's *1984* and omnipresent video surveillance. But biometrics, like any technology, is morally neutral. Any abuses will stem from the human element in our government. And biometric systems could help to control, counter and check those error-prone human elements.

Strictly speaking, what is a biometric system? A biometric system used personal traits or physical characteristics to recognize an individual. The signature on the back of our credit cards is a very primitive biometric; so is any photo ID or mug shot. The human optic nerve is hooked to our brain's biological facial-recognition database. Bloodhounds track trails of unique individual scents.

Examples of more-advanced biometric systems in use include a facial-recognition system used by the West Virginia Department of Motor Vehicles to scan applicants for duplicate or fraudulent driver's licenses. The state of Georgia now includes a digital thumbprint on its licenses. Typing and mouse-use patterns also can be used to identify individuals, existing technology likely to be deployed online. Predictive Networks, a Cambridge, Mass., company, has developed software to do just that. High-tech spy thrillers on television and in the movies have acquainted us with the retinal scans, voice prints and hand-geometry scanners just beginning to be deployed. The gambling industry is considering the use of voice-recognition technology to control access to telephone gambling networks, for example. Less-familiar biometric systems include earlobe analysis and body-odor sniffers. But widespread deployment of biometric systems still is part of sci-fi future.

In that future, the trends suggest that biometrics will be a boon to privacy and security in the private sector. In the works is voice-print technology that will recognize only authorized users of long-distance telephone services or brokerage accounts, keeping out snoops. Handprints and iris scans can make it harder for hackers to fool computer networks, expanding the realm of possibility for authorized computer users safely to access sensitive medical records or other data remotely. Thieves of portable items such as cell phones, laptops, cars and credit cards will find their booty useless without the rightful owner's fingerprints to activate them. Most people have trouble remembering the long combinations of random letters and numbers needed for a really secure password. the digital record of one's fingerprints, though, can be scrambled into a unique personal-identification number to foil identity thieves. As the cost of this technology comes down and its accuracy is improved, widespread deployment in the private sector is almost a given wherever current identification systems lag behind security needs.

Safeguards for Citizens

What of the use of biometrics in and by government? Some civil libertarians fear a controlled government database chock-full of biometric data and a nationwide system of scanners and controls from which there is no escape. Religious, political or racial minorities could be hunted down. Rogue police could harass innocents that unwittingly have offended them.

Will biometrics facilitate human-rights violations on a trivial or massive scale? The short answer is it could do either, but the risk is no greater than for any other modern identification technology. And it can be controlled. The choice we have is not between zero-risk and risky identification systems. It is a choice between the current systems, which do not prevent government abuses and yet are fraught with security holes and other problems, or more effective modern systems no more liable to abuse than any other.

> **Declaring certain technologies off-limits would not resolve the danger of abuse and would prevent government from effectively carrying out legitimate functions.**

The present reality is that the current system of identification, based on the Social Security number, signature and driver's license, has failed. In a world of open public records and long-distance financial transactions over electronic networks, the Social Security number cannot continue to function as a password. The driver's license cannot be displayed as proof of age or identity over a network. Most importantly for the evolution of systems of identification, the current system has failed to provide the degree of protection against fraud that consumers would like to have. It is proving inadequate for legitimate law-enforcement purposes as well, especially as criminals have increased mobility across jurisdictions. These legitimate purposes of law enforcement include everyday protection against ordinary criminals as well as rarer terrorist events.

One way or another, current methods of authentication must be replaced or augmented—perhaps with digital signatures, perhaps with better biometrics (the photo ID and signature already are biometrics of a weak, error-prone sort) or perhaps with some combination.

Any system of information collection is subject to abuse. Data collected by the national census can be abused, and was when data was used during World War II to relocate Japanese-Americans. Wiretapping has been abused. Even the technology built into cell phones to help authorities pinpoint the locations of 911 callers could be used for nefarious purposes by an evil regime to track innocent people.

The dangers and history of government abuses are real. But at the same time they are highly speculative. Given the reality of abuses and their relative rarity in the modern U.S. context, where do we draw the line? The risk that imperfect systems of identification will provide opportunities for fraud, terrorism and other crimes also is real. And these acts, too, violate our rights to security of life and limb as well as property rights. Do we know that the benefits of "leaky" systems in allowing dissidents additional leeway along with criminals will outweigh the costs? The answer probably is different at different times and places throughout history. We only can make a best guess.

Do we say, as our rule of thumb, that the government may not collect or use biometric data? That some technologies simply will be off-limits to law enforcement? This would be both unrealistic and ineffective.

Some danger of abuse, however remote, extends to any technology wielded by government. Adolf Hitler and Josef Stalin managed to create a nightmare world without any electronic biometrics at all. Human beings (neighborhood informants) also can serve as surveillance for low-tech totalitarian police, as in Communist China. Declaring certain technologies off-limits would not resolve the danger of abuse and would prevent government from effectively carrying out legitimate functions.

Checks and Balances

If the answer to preserving freedom is not in declaring certain technology off-limits, where does the answer lie? The battle to preserve civil liberties and rights is more about institutions and legal rights and powers than about this or that technology. The Fourth Amendment does not say that the government may not collect, keep or store information. It says the police must show probable cause and obtain a warrant from a judge to conduct a search. The police are made accountable to the judiciary. This is an institutional solution, an accountability solution, going back to the old idea of checks and balances. Other constitutional principles—the freedom of speech, protection against the confiscation of private property, the right to a jury trial and constitutional protections against torture and cruel and unusual punishments—work together to hold back the human tendencies of those who govern to take more power than we willingly would give.

Indeed, biometrics promise to make government more accountable and less likely to misuse private information. Suppose biometrics technology were used to restrict the access of government employees to citizens' tax records, criminal records and other files. Logs show which government employees access the files and when. Victims of rogue employees in government offices would stand a better chance of finding who had accessed their records and holding the rogues accountable. Illicit access by hackers coming from outside the system also would be reduced.

Because biometrics can help reduce the incidence of fraud and help police track perpetrators of violence in the most high-risk zones, such as airports and nuclear facilities, it may help preserve an open society in other areas. People terrified that criminals lurk among them undetected are not people who will embrace freedom. So long as our law-enforcement networks do not meaningfully help police target and quickly identify wrongdoers, we all will have to endure more random searches, generalized surveillance and heavy regulation.

The key to preserving our liberties does not lie with declaring biometrics off-limits for governments or anyone else. It lies in the realm of ideas and beliefs, powers and rights. Authoritarianism is not a gadget, it is a state of mind.

11

The Government May Use New Data-Mining Technology to Breach Privacy Rights

Max Blumenthal

Max Blumenthal is a writer living in Los Angeles.

In the fight against terrorism, America's national security agencies are researching new supercomputer and satellite technologies that would allow them to continually search through billions of credit card and bank statements, rental agreements, and dozens of other personal documents. This "data-mining" technology could be used to violate constitutional protections against unreasonable searches and has upset critics on both the left and the right. Few Americans want the government reading their e-mails, checking into their spending habits, or snooping through their medical records. People are also concerned that data-mining systems will generate "false positives"—people conducting seemingly suspicious activities who prove to be innocent. Despite the potential dangers, the government and private companies have been secretive about their data-mining initiatives. In a democratic society, people have the right to know that their private affairs are being monitored by government spies.

Max Blumenthal, "Data Debase: The Powerful Technology Known as Data Mining—and How, in the Government's Hands, It Could Become a Civil Libertarian's Nightmare," *The American Prospect*, December 19, 2003. Copyright © 2003 by The American Prospect, Inc., 11 Beacon St., Suite 1120, Boston, MA 02108. All rights reserved. Reproduced by permission.

S teven Spielberg's 2002 film *Minority Report* depicted a futur-
istic dystopia in which a "Department of Pre-Crime" jails
people for acts they haven't yet committed. In an apparent case
of life imitating art, Spielberg's Shoah Foundation—a nonprofit
[corporation] the film director established in 1994 to videotape
and preserve the testimonies of Holocaust survivors—has
handed over the words of 51,000 Holocaust survivors to aid a
team of government-funded researchers in developing a revo-
lutionary technology inspired by elements of the Pentagon's
scuttled domestic-surveillance program, Terrorism Information
Awareness (TIA).

TIA, which was blocked by Congress, was to have been a mix
of high-tech voice-recognition and data-mining programs that
would have made up the largest domestic-surveillance system in
the United States. Using TIA, intelligence analysts and law-
enforcement officials would have been able to trawl through
Americans' private records—including banking transactions, e-
mail accounts and travel records, such as plane ticket information—in order to finger terrorists. Though TIA would have been
composed largely of voice-recognition surveillance programs, it
was the proposal's reliance on the new science of data mining
that had groups from the American Civil Liberties Union to the
archconservative Free Congress Foundation up in arms.

> *Data mining seeks to classify a person's threat
> level according to superficial patterns of activity like
> bank withdrawals and travel history.*

Broadly speaking, data mining is an innovation of statistical science that allows analysts to detect patterns of events and
relationships in order to discover a "gem," or a hidden fact. The
idea is to allow users to accurately forecast future events. When
data mining emerged in the late 1990s, MIT's [Massachusetts
Institute of Technology's] *Technology Review* hailed it as one of
the 10 new technologies that will "change the world." Since
then, data mining has revolutionized everything from how
companies monitor customers' online purchasing habits to
how the federal government practices counterterrorism.

Data-mining advocates within the law-enforcement and intelligence communities claim the science makes retrieval of ex-

isting information more convenient, allowing them to identify and track terrorists without costly and time-consuming legwork. However, data-mining programs like TIA—which would have allowed analysts to sift through private citizens' personal records without a search warrant in order to identify patterns that would suggest terrorist activity—pose some pretty serious due-process problems. Data mining seeks to classify a person's threat level according to superficial patterns of activity like bank withdrawals and travel history. Supporters say this is useful because terrorists typically lead transient lifestyles and have spotty pasts. But so do homeless people, migrant workers and more than a few journalists. Perhaps the most troubling aspect of data mining is that it offers the government a convenient tool to analyze individuals' political and religious affiliations by investigating library records, magazine subscriptions and group memberships. Of course, there is no indication that this is actually happening, but it is a possibility that civil-liberties advocates worry about.

Bush Backs Programs

Though Congress elected to defund TIA—in a nearly unanimous Sept. 24 [2004] vote on defense budget appropriations—the Bush administration is backing a series of TIA-inspired data-mining programs set for implementation by other government agencies and private companies. The Department of Homeland Security's Transportation Security Agency [TSA] is planning to employ an airline-security program . . . called Customer Assisted Passenger Profiling II (CAPPS II), which will use data mining to assign color codes to passengers based on their potential threat levels. A private data-mining company, Seisint Inc., has received funding from the departments of Justice and Homeland Security for a program called Multistate Anti-Terrorism Information Exchange (MATRIX), which is set for implementation in five states. And the National Science Foundation (NSF) is funding a data-mining project—led by university researchers and Spielberg's Shoah Foundation—that would allow users to index massive audio recordings by specific spoken words or phrases.

And TIA itself has not really gone away. In July [2004] as the Senate seemed poised to ban data-mining programs entirely, the White House's Office of Budget and Management protested the restriction of what it called "a powerful potential tool in the war on terrorism," stating, "The administration urges the Senate to remove the provision that prohibits any research and development for the Terrorism Information Awareness [TIA] program." As a result of White House pressure, the bill ultimately agreed upon by a joint House-Senate appropriations committee made allowances for TIA's voice-recognition programs to continue in a research-and-development phase at the Pentagon, while its data-mining programs were transferred to the National Foreign Intelligence Program (NFIP), an agency with a classified budget jointly managed by the CIA, FBI and National Security Agency (NSA). The bill also glaringly avoided the term "data mining," instead authorizing the NFIP to employ "processing, analysis and collaboration tools for counterterrorism foreign intelligence." And the committee limited the NFIP to tracking "noncitizens"—meaning, in effect, that foreigners living and working in the United States are still subject to being tracked by TIA. . . .

So TIA's most controversial features live on, though in a limited scope and shrouded in the thick of a bureaucratic wilderness. Case in point: The Pentagon's Counterintelligence Field Activity division, a group that works to protect the Defense Department and its personnel from espionage threats, has recently been charged with conducting a data-mining mission, which, according to the *Los Angeles Times'* William Arkin, includes "process[ing] massive sets of public records, intercepted communications, credit card accounts, etc., to find 'actionable intelligence.'"

As David Sobel, general counsel of the Electronic Privacy Information Center, told me, the bevy of data-mining surveillance programs popping up in government agencies is a trend that will continue to be difficult to monitor. "At the moment there is no government-wide restriction on what we commonly think of as data mining," Sobel explained. "Similar programs and the development of related technologies are likely to be driven underground, and at the moment I don't think there's a very good sense on what those initiatives might be."

Tracking Airline Passengers

Information has surfaced recently revealing that one of the government's major data-mining initiatives, CAPPS II, was developed largely "underground" with the help of private corporations unaccountable to the public. It is not known exactly when CAPPS II's development was initiated, though the program likely began in December 2001, when, according to *The Washington Times*, NASA's Aviation Systems Division obtained more than 15 million private passenger records from Northwest Airlines after a secret meeting between officials from the two organizations. According to documents obtained by the *Times* in August 2002, NASA officials solicited Northwest's records for use as research data in developing what would have amounted to a mind-reading device. NASA proposed in these documents to detect and analyze passengers' brainwaves, heartbeat rates and eye-flicker rates and correlate them with data on their travel routines, criminal background and credit information from "hundreds to thousands of data sources" to "determine who is a threat."

> **//**At the moment there is no government-wide restriction on what we commonly think of as data mining.**//**

Though NASA's bizarre proposal has yet to come to fruition, the development of a strikingly similar program came to light this September [2003], when Jet Blue Airlines admitted to handing over the personal records of 5 million customers in early 2002 to Torch Concepts, a private data-mining contractor hired by the Defense Department. TSA officials have subsequently admitted that they facilitated the handover of Jet Blue's records to Torch; they told *Wired News* that the study was for a program to improve security on U.S. Army bases.

However, a look at Torch's test, which bears no mention of the military, suggests something altogether different. According to Torch documents discovered online by travel privacy activist Edward Hasbrouck, the test correlated Jet Blue customers' records with their Social Security numbers, income levels and home ownership statuses to group customers into one of three categories based on their perceived threat level: young, middle-income homeowners; older, upper-income homeowners; and a group of passengers with "anomalous" records.

Torch's method of classification looks like a blueprint for CAPPS II, which would require airline passengers to provide carriers with their home addresses, phone numbers and dates of birth for entry in[to] a government-administered computer system. That information would be correlated with government and commercial data, including bank account information and travel records. Finally, passengers would be placed in one of three color-coded categories based on their perceived threat levels. Those deemed "anomalous" in Torch's experiment would have been assigned a yellow code under CAPPS II and subjected to additional security checks; those judged nonthreatening would earn a green code and board smoothly; and those whose names showed up on a watch list would be labeled red and then barred from flying or arrested.

As with TIA, CAPPS II has renewed the debate in Congress over the appropriate place of data mining in a democratic society. Led by the technology's staunchest opponent on Capitol Hill, Sen. Ron Wyden (D-Ore.), lawmakers have taken steps to further restrict its use, making CAPPS II's funding in the Homeland Security appropriations bill contingent on a favorable review by the General Accounting Office, which is preparing a report on the program's ability to differentiate between terrorists and innocent people.

The MATRIX Program

Congress has no jurisdiction, however, to oversee another TIA-like program developed by private Boca Raton, Fla., technology firm Seisint Inc. for use by state governments. Seisint's MATRIX program is essentially a scaled-down version of TIA that uses data mining to establish links between people and patterns of events. *The Washington Post* reported that the system would be able to "find the name and address of every brown-haired owner of a red Ford pickup truck in a 20-mile radius of a suspicious event." But precisely because of the program's near-omniscient power, even Florida's special agent in charge of statewide intelligence is worried. As he told the *Post*, "It's scary. It could be abused. I mean, I can call up everything about you, your pictures and pictures of your neighbors."

MATRIX has been in use in Florida for more than a year and in August [2003], the Department of Homeland Security announced plans to incorporate nearly a dozen states into the program. MATRIX is the creation of former alleged drug smuggler Hank Asher, who, according to the *Post*, boasted to Florida police officials in the wake of the September 11 attacks that he could develop a system to find the hijackers and any terrorists who might strike in the future. Since Asher initiated the program, Seisint, of which he is CEO, has received a $4 million grant from the Department of Justice and an $8 million pledge from the Department of Homeland Security, a signal of the federal government's determination to spread the program nationwide. Indeed, as reported by the *Post*, in a Jan. 26, 2003, speech to the Florida Sheriffs Winter Conference, state Commissioner of Law Enforcement James Moore called MATRIX the "first step in developing a national intelligence network."

> *// NASA proposed . . . to detect and analyze passengers' brainwaves, heartbeat rates and eye-flicker rates and correlate them with data on their travel routines, criminal background and credit information. //*

If deployed throughout the country, a program such as MA-TRIX would give local police officers the same power to snoop through individuals' personal records and analyze data that Pentagon anti-terrorism experts would have enjoyed with TIA. According to MATRIX's Web site, this would mean prying into an individual's criminal history, driver's license data, vehicle-registration records and incarceration records, including digitized photographs "with significant amounts of public data record entries." Because the site does not specify which type of "public data record entries" are to be searched, there is no assurance against the investigation of magazine subscriptions, library records and group affiliations—political, religious or otherwise.

Speech Recognition

Meanwhile, the National Science Foundation and the Shoah Foundation are developing a technology that would give users the power to search through large recordings of speech in any of 32 languages to instantly find a given word or phrase. To develop this technology, called Multilingual Access to Large Spoken Archives (MALACH), the NSF earmarked $7.5 million in 2001 to Shoah and a team of university computer scientists. Today, MALACH is one of the most ambitious and highly funded programs in the Networking and Information Technology Research and Development Program—a group with a $5 billion annual budget that NSF administers, along with agencies like the Defense Advanced Research Projects Agency (DARPA) and the NSA—to create new indexing, information-retrieval and data-mining technology. (NSF's MALACH administrator, Saul Greenspan, declined to be interviewed for this article.)

According to press releases from the Shoah Foundation and the University of Maryland Institute for Advanced Computational Studies (UMIACS), which is spearheading MALACH's research, the impetus for developing MALACH came from Shoah, which was struggling to index 116,000 hours of digitally archived videotape testimony from more than 51,000 Holocaust survivors (many of whom are still alive). So far, at its Los Angeles museum, Shoah has managed to index only 4,000 individual testimonies at a whopping cost of $8 million. An audio search engine like MALACH would make the indexing process a walk in the park, which is why Shoah turned over its entire archive of Holocaust testimonies to MALACH's research team for use as a data set to test the technology.

> **"** It's scary. It could be abused. I mean, I can call up everything about you, your pictures and pictures of your neighbors. **"**

However, with such a large grant from the NSF, it would be naive to assume that MALACH is an altruistic gift to Shoah. Indeed, a UMIACS press release acknowledges that "this technology will produce significant impact, both through improved access to our cultural heritage and through the application of the techniques that we will develop to other important problems." Whether those "other important problems" include terrorism does not concern Sam Gustman, Shoah's technology director and a former information-retrieval specialist from the Army Corps of Engineers. "If the results of the National Science Foundation project are used by other projects, it's public," Gustman told me. "Our goal is to help the [NSF] further the state-of-the-art technology. Now, if someone uses that [technology] for something else, well, that's the effect of working on something in the public domain."

One of MALACH's lead researchers is Douglas Oard of

the University of Maryland, an information-retrieval and automated-translation specialist who is also an expert in high-tech counterterrorism applications. His expertise earned him a grant from DARPA's Information Awareness Office to develop an Arabic and Chinese automatic translation program called TIDES (Translingual Information Detection, Extraction and Summarization), which was to be a major component of TIA. Oard also participated in a recent DARPA project to develop tools to translate Hindi into English. And he has taught a seminar at the University of Maryland called "Information Technology and the War on Terror."

Asked about MALACH's origins, Oard says the program grew out of his earlier work for DARPA developing TIA. As he told me, MALACH "takes some of the research from TIDES, the DARPA program, and it applies it to a National Science Foundation program." Oard would not address MALACH's potential application to the war on terrorism directly, but he did make clear that it could have a broad societal impact. "If you could [implement MALACH], it would change a lot of things—and we're making very good progress—about how we do things in our society," Oard said. "Recording conversations is not hard to do, but using the recorded conversation is extremely difficult. So we're trying to make tools that will help you with that. As soon as we do that, we will have changed a fundamental assumption in our society that speech is ephemeral. This could very well revolutionize the way in which our society treats speech."

Just as data mining gives analysts the power to dig through anything from someone's travel records to their Department of Motor Vehicles files for a valuable piece of information, MALACH would allow them to do the same with recorded speech. Considering that thousands of hours of speech are recorded each week in dozens of languages through surveillance satellites and wiretaps by agencies like the NSA, the speed and convenience that MALACH would afford investigators in searching for specific words and phrases is likely to lower the threshold on government snooping.

Oard is surprisingly frank on the question of whether the technology he is developing provides cause for concern. "It's not worth worrying about as a developer," he said. "As a member of society it's very worth worrying about."

12

The Government Is Designing Data-Mining Technology That Will Protect Privacy Rights

Tony Tether

Tony Tether is the director of the Defense Advanced Research Projects Agency (DARPA).

After the terrorist attacks on the Pentagon and World Trade Center on September 11, 2001, the Department of Defense created the Defense Advanced Research Projects Agency, or DARPA. The mission of this agency is to develop tools for data mining, a process of using technology to comb through billions of personal and business records in the attempt to identify terrorists. Although civil libertarians fear that privacy will be violated by these searches, DARPA is taking every precaution to protect privacy rights. Instead of conducting vast random searches of individual records, the new technology is based on developing attack scenarios or hypotheses about terrorist plans. The government would use these scenarios to focus its data mining on the records of plausible suspects. The technology also has built-in safeguards to prevent abuse by those who would use surveillance for personal or political reasons. While some are frightened by the thought of government agents looking at their financial statements, medical records, and other personal data, DARPA's mission is to stop terrorism, not invade personal privacy. As this

Tony Tether, statement before the U.S. House Subcommittee on Technology, Information Policy, Intergovernmental Relations, and the Census, Committee on Government Reform, Washington, DC, May 6, 2003.

developing technology is employed, America—and the world—will be a safer place.

Editor's note: The following is excerpted from a statement given by Tether before the U.S. House of Representatives on May 6, 2003.

I am Tony Tether, Director of the Defense Advanced Research Projects Agency (DARPA). I am pleased to appear before you today to talk about data mining and protecting the privacy of Americans. This is an important issue, and I hope that you will find my remarks helpful as your subcommittee looks into this complicated topic.

Some of you might be unfamiliar with DARPA. We are, essentially, tool makers, sponsoring high-payoff research for the Department of Defense (DoD). This research includes several new software tools that DARPA is developing to assist the DoD in its counterterrorism mission. We are developing new data search and pattern recognition technologies, which have little in common with existing data mining technology, and represent just one element of DARPA's counterterrorism research. Other critical areas of our research include secure collaborative problem solving, structured knowledge discovery, data visualization, and decision making with corporate memory.

It is important to remember that the technologies I will be discussing do not yet exist in their final form, and, no doubt, they will change. Some will succeed and some will fail, and we will learn as we go along. That is the nature of research.

Moreover, unlike some of the other agencies represented by my fellow panelists today, DARPA is not an agency that will actually use these tools, if they work. Other agencies in the DoD, Federal government, or Congress will decide if they want to use the tools we create and how they will use them.

Data Search and Pattern Recognition

When most people talk about "data mining," they are referring to the use of clever statistical techniques to comb through large amounts of data to discover previously unknown, but useful patterns for building predictive models. This is typically done in the commercial world to better predict customer purchases, understand supply chains, or find fraud—or address any number of other issues where a better understanding of behavior patterns would be helpful. The basic approach is to find statistical correlations as a means of discovering unknown behavior patterns, and then build a predictive model.

At first, one might think that data mining would be very helpful for the most general attempts to find terrorists. It would appear ideal to have software that could automatically discover suspicious, but previously unnoticed patterns in large amounts of data, and which could be used to create models for "connecting-the-dots" and predicting attacks beforehand. However, there are fundamental limitations to expanding today's data mining approaches to the challenge of generally finding and interdicting complex and meticulously well-planned terrorist plots that involve various individuals.

> ❝ To detect and prevent complex terrorist plots, one must find extremely rare instances of patterns across an extremely wide variety of activities—and hidden relationships among individuals. ❞

Skeptics believe that such techniques are not feasible because it is simply too difficult to program software to answer the general question, "Is that activity suspicious?" when terrorist plans are so variable and evidence of them is so rare. The results, skeptics say, will contain unmanageable numbers of "false positives"—activities flagged as suspicious that turn out to be innocent.

Beyond the skeptics, critics claim that such an approach must inevitably lead to "fishing expeditions" through massive amounts of personal data and a wholesale invasion of Americans' privacy that yields, basically, nothing in terms of finding terrorists. In previous testimony, this approach has been referred to as "mass dataveillance."

In fact, these objections are among the reasons why DARPA is not pursuing these techniques, but is developing a different approach in our research.

DARPA is *not* trying to bring about "mass dataveillance," regardless of what you have read or heard. We believe that the existing data mining approach of discovering previously unknown patterns is ill-suited to ferreting out terrorist plans.

The purpose of data mining is, typically, to find previously unknown but useful patterns of behavior in large amounts of data on activities that are narrowly defined and identified, such as credit card usage or book purchases. These behavior patterns relate to individual transactions or classes of transactions (but not to individuals, themselves), again in narrowly defined and identified areas of activity.

> *// The focus is* investigative *as opposed to broad surveillance. //*

The counterterrorism problem is much more difficult than this. To detect and prevent complex terrorist plots, one must find *extremely rare* instances of patterns across an *extremely wide* variety of activities—and *hidden* relationships among individuals. Data mining is ill-suited to this task because the domains of potentially interesting activity are so much more numerous and complex than purchasing behavior.

Accordingly, we believe that better tools and a different approach are needed for the most general efforts to detect and prevent complicated, well-planned terrorist plots, particularly if we are to prevent them well before they can occur and long before they can reach U.S. shores. Consequently, our research goal to create better counterterrorism tools will not be realized by surveilling huge piles of data representing a collection of broad or ill-defined activities in the hope of discovering previously unknown, unspecified patterns. Instead, we are pursuing an approach of searching for *evidence* of specified patterns.

Detecting Data That Fits Specified Patterns

Our approach starts with developing attack scenarios, which are used to find specific patterns that could indicate terrorist plans or planning. These scenarios would be based on expert knowledge from previous terrorist attacks, intelligence analysis, new information about terrorist techniques, and/or from wargames in which clever people imagine ways to attack the United States and its deployed forces. The basic approach does not rely on statistical analysis to discover unknown patterns for creating predictive models. Instead, we start with expert knowledge to create scenarios in support of intelligence analysis versus a data mining approach that scans databases for previously unknown correlations.

The scenarios would then be reduced to a series of questions about which data would provide evidence that such attacks were being planned. We call these scenarios "models," and they are, essentially, hypotheses about terrorist plans. Our goal is to detect data that supports the hypotheses.

Contrast this approach with trying to discover a suspicious pattern without having a model as a starting point—when the pattern is not known in advance. Consider a truck bomb attack, involving a rental truck filled with fertilizer and other materials. Trying to get software to discover such an attack in its planning stages by combing through piles of data—not knowing what it was looking for, but trying to flag "suspicious" activities suggestive of terrorist planning—is unlikely to work. Terrorist activity is far too rare, and spotting it across many different activities by broadly surveilling all available data requires enormous knowledge about the world in order to identify an activity or individual as being "suspicious."

> *// DARPA's research seeks to provide analysts with powerful tools, not replace the analysts themselves. //*

DARPA's approach, instead, focuses a search on detecting evidence for the scenario model or hypothesis, "Are there foreign visitors to the United States who are staying in urban areas, buying large amounts of fertilizer and renting trucks?" Again, the model or hypothesis is not created by meandering through vast amounts of data to discover unknown patterns.

Finding the evidence of a suspicious pattern is, of course, not as simple as I have made it sound. DARPA's counterterrorism research in the areas of data search and pattern recognition is based on two basic types of queries that, as a practical matter, would probably be used in combination.

The first type of query is subject-based and begins with an entity, such as people *known* to be suspects. Analysts would start with actual suspects' names and see if there is evidence of links with other suspects or suspicious activities. Current technology and policy pertaining to subject-based queries are fairly well developed and understood. One method of subject-based query with enormous potential is link analysis, which seeks to discover knowledge based on the relationships in data about people, places, things, and events. Link analysis makes it possible to understand the relationships between entities. Properly assembled, these links can provide a picture of higher-level terrorist networks and activities, which, in turn, forms a basis for early indications and warning of a terror attack. Data mining offers little as a tool for investigating such relationships—it creates models by finding statistical correlations within databases without using a starting point, and then applies these models indiscriminately over entire data sets. Link analysis differs because it detects connectedness within rare patterns using known starting points, reducing the search space at the outset.

The second type of query is strictly pattern-based. Analysts would look for evidence of a specified pattern of activity that might be a threat.

It is crucial to note that both types of queries start with either known, identified suspects or known, identified patterns. The focus is *investigative* as opposed to broad surveillance. In both cases, the data that one is looking for is likely to be distributed over a large number of very different databases. Querying distributed, heterogeneous databases is not easy, particularly if we are trying to detect patterns, and we do not know how to do it right now. Pattern query technology is a critical element of our counterterrorism research; it is rather immature, as are the policies governing its application.

The data that analysts get back in response to a query might not tell them everything. The response may depend on who is doing the analysis and their levels of authorization. This brings me to the second aspect of our approach, detecting in stages.

Detecting in Stages

We envision that analysts will search for evidence of specified patterns in stages. They will ask questions, get some results, and then refine their results by asking more questions. This is really just common sense, but it is worth highlighting that detecting in stages offers a number of advantages: it uses information more efficiently; it helps limit false positives; it can conform to legal investigative procedures; and it allows privacy protection to be built-in.

Detecting in stages helps deal with the crucial challenge of false positives—that is, mistakenly flagging activities and people as suspicious that are, in fact, innocuous. False positives waste investigative resources and, in the worst cases, can lead to false accusations. Unfortunately, much of the discussion of false positives and counterterrorism has tended to emphasize technology as the key issue by implicitly assuming a caricature of an investigative process in which a computer program fishes through massive piles of data, officials press the "print" button, and out pop a bunch of arrest warrants. Of course, such an approach is unworkable.

> *We knew that the American public and their elected officials must have confidence that their liberties will not be violated before they would accept this kind of technology.*

We recognize that false positives must be considered as a product of the whole system. They result from how the data, the technology, the personnel, *and* the investigative procedures interact with each other—they are not solely the result of the application of less-than-perfect technology. DARPA's research seeks to provide analysts with powerful tools, not replace the analysts themselves. Moreover, how we react to positives and what we plan to do with the result is what matters enormously to this issue.

It is also important to remember that all investigations—whether they use databases or not—will yield false positives. Therefore, the relevant question is, "Can we improve our overall ability to detect and prevent terrorist attacks without having an unacceptable false positive rate at the system level?" That is the key challenge to be answered by our research.

No doubt many of the "positives" found during the first queries that analysts make will be false ones. The positives must be further examined to start weeding out the false ones and confirming the real ones, if there are any. This will require analysis in several stages to find independent, additional evidence that either refutes or continues to support the hypothesis represented by the model. Moreover, the level of proof depends, in part, on the nature of the planned response to a positive. We do not, for example, arrest everyone who sets off the metal detector when entering this building.

An analogy we sometimes use to illustrate this is submarine detection. In submarine warfare, we do not simply attack something based on first indications that a single sensor has detected an object. We refine the object's identification in stages—from "possible" enemy submarine, to "probable" enemy submarine, to "certainly" an enemy submarine. To be sure of our actions, we confirm the identification over time, using different, independent sensors and sources of information. Our approach to data searching and pattern recognition would proceed in a similar fashion.

Proceeding in stages also means that the entire process can conform to required, legal procedures or steps. In fact, many of these steps exist *precisely* to protect people's rights and weed out false positives. We envision hard-wiring many of the required procedures, permissions, or business rules into the software to ensure that they are actually being followed at each stage of the process.

Let us go back to the truck bomb example. One might incorporate a process called "selective revelation" into data queries. In selective revelation, the amount of information revealed to the analyst depends on who the analyst is, the status of the investigation, and the specific authorization the analyst has received. The analyst's credentials would be automatically included with the query, and the level of information returned would vary accordingly.

Perhaps the result of the truck bomb query I talked about earlier is that 17 people fit the truck bomber pattern, but no personal information about those 17 is revealed. To retrieve additional personal information, a higher level of authorization might be required, based on an independent evaluation (by a court, for example) of the evidence that the analyst is actually "on to" something suspicious.

This suggests that there is a special class of business rules and procedures that could be put into the technology to strengthen privacy protection, so let me turn to that now.

Built-in Privacy Protection

From the very start of our research, we began looking for ways to build privacy protection into DARPA's approach to detecting terrorists.

We had two motivations. First, we knew that the American

public and their elected officials must have confidence that their liberties will not be violated before they would accept this kind of technology.

Second, much of what Federal agencies need to share is *intelligence* data. Historically, agencies have been reluctant to share intelligence data for fear of exposing their sources and methods. Accordingly, protecting privacy and intelligence sources and methods are integral to our approach.

> *DARPA is, in fact, one of the few Federal agencies sponsoring significant research in the area of privacy protection technologies.*

We are putting policies into place that will highlight protecting privacy. As I previously alluded, DARPA does not own or collect any intelligence or law enforcement databases. Our policies will address the development and transition of new tools to the agencies authorized by law to use those databases, reinforcing to everyone the importance of privacy. . . .

To further assist agencies that have collected the data for analysis, we are developing other tools that will help them protect the integrity of the information—even during searches. I previously mentioned "selective revelation" as one way to protect privacy, and we are looking at other related techniques as well, such as separating identity information from transaction information. These separate pieces of information could only be reassembled after the analyst has received the proper authorizations.

Until then, an analyst might only know the basic facts but not the identity of who was involved. We are also looking at ways to anonymize data before it is analyzed. We are evaluating methods for filtering out irrelevant information from the analysis, such as the use of "software agents" that utilize experience-based rules. These software agents would automatically remove data that appears to be irrelevant before the analyst even sees it.

Going beyond privacy protection, we are also looking into building-in indelible audit technology that makes it exceedingly difficult to abuse the data search and pattern recognition technology without the abuse being detected. This audit technology would answer the question, "Who used the system to retrieve what data?"

Some ideas that we are pursuing include cryptographically protecting audit information and perhaps even broadcasting it to outside parties, where it cannot be tampered with. We are also looking into software agents that would watch what analysts are doing to ensure that their searches and procedures are appropriate and that they are following established guidelines.

Another interesting idea is data that reports its location back to the system. One might even include a unique identifier for each copy ("digital watermark"), so that if unauthorized copies were distributed their source could be traced. Still another concept is giving control of database querying a trusted third party, who could not be subject to organizational pressure to provide unauthorized access.

We take privacy issues very seriously. DARPA is, in fact, one of the few Federal agencies sponsoring significant research in the area of privacy protection technologies.

You will often hear talk in this debate about how there are trade-offs—for instance, that we may need to trade less privacy for more security. People may disagree about the proper balance, but DARPA's efforts in developing privacy protection technology are designed, in fact, to improve prospects for providing both improved privacy protection and improved security by the legally relevant agencies.

In closing, I would like to emphasize two points:

First, remember that what I have been describing here today is research, and exactly how the technology will work—indeed, *if* it works—will only be shown over time.

Second, because of the high profile of DARPA's research in this area, in February 2003 the Department of Defense announced the establishment of two boards to provide oversight of our Information Awareness programs, including our data search and pattern recognition technologies. These two boards, an internal oversight board and an outside advisory committee, will work with DARPA as we proceed with our research to ensure full compliance with U.S. constitutional law, U.S. statutory law, and American values related to privacy.

13

The Patriot Act Gives the FBI Unchecked Power to Spy on Ordinary Citizens

American Civil Liberties Union

The American Civil Liberties Union works in courts, legislatures, and communities to defend and protect the individual rights and liberties guaranteed by the Constitution and laws of the United States.

After the terrorist attacks of September 11, 2001, Congress passed the USA PATRIOT Act. Several provisions of the act give the Federal Bureau of Investigation (FBI) unprecedented powers to violate privacy rights guaranteed by the U.S. Constitution. The part of the act known as Section 215, for example, gives FBI agents the right to look at people's medical records, read their e-mails, check out the Web sites they have visited, investigate their religious affiliations, and even see which books they have checked out of the library. People forced to turn over these personal records, such as librarians and doctors, are required by law to tell no one—ever—under threat of felony prosecution. Section 215 might be used to catch suspected terrorists, but it could also be used against protesters, political enemies, or anyone else. The FBI has a well-documented history of abusing its authority, dating back to the 1950s. While the threat of terrorism is real, giving unchecked powers to secret government investigators is no way to stop it.

American Civil Liberties Union, "Unpatriotic Acts: The FBI's Power to Rifle Through Your Records and Personal Belongings Without Telling You," www. aclu.org, July 2003. Copyright © 2003 by the American Civil Liberties Union. Reproduced by permission.

I magine this scenario: You flee Iraq after being imprisoned and persecuted for your political views. When you arrive in the United States, a local charity helps you find housing and medical care. You start a small business, join a mosque, and become active in a Muslim community association. You use email at a public library to keep in touch with your extended family in Iraq, and to discuss politics with friends. Two years later, you are grateful for the freedoms you enjoy in your new home.

> **//** *Section 215 . . . lets the government obtain personal records or things about* anyone—*from libraries, Internet service providers, hospitals, or any business.* **//**

When the U.S. invades Iraq, you are thankful to be rid of Saddam but angry about civilian casualties and the extended U.S. occupation. You write a letter to the editor of your local newspaper encouraging a quick transfer of power to Iraqi civilians.

An FBI agent who is conducting an investigation of other Iraqi-Americans notices your letter and finds it troubling. Based on the letter, the sound of your name, and the outside possibility that you may be connected to the people he's investigating, he decides to investigate you. He goes to a secret court and gets an order that forces the library and its Internet service provider to turn over all your email messages. Then he gets another secret order to obtain records from the charity that helped you when you first arrived in the United States. Those records lead him to the local hospital, where he obtains records of medical treatment you received. He serves another order on the local mosque to find out whether or not you're a member or serve in a leadership position. Though he uncovered nothing suspicious about you in his fishing expedition, he gets another secret order forcing the Muslim community association to turn over its entire membership list. If not you, he thinks, maybe another member has some connection to those people he's investigating. . . .

As it turns out, you never learn that the FBI is spying on you. The FBI certainly doesn't tell you. And the library, the charity, the hospital, the mosque, and the community association are all prohibited—forever—from telling you or anyone else that the FBI has asked for your records. You simply never learn that the government has been rifling through your life.

Could such a thing happen to you or someone you know? Perhaps it already has. The USA PATRIOT Act vastly expands the FBI's authority to monitor people living in the United States. These powers can be used not only against terrorists and spies but also against ordinary, law-abiding people—immigrants from Iraq or Italy, dentists from Detroit or Denver, truck drivers from Tampa or Tulsa, painters from Peoria or Pittsburgh. Indeed, the FBI can use these powers to spy on *any* United States citizen or resident.

This report examines in detail one PATRIOT Act provision, Section 215, which gives the FBI unprecedented access to sensitive, personal records and any "tangible things." The report explains why Section 215 is misguided, dangerous, and unconstitutional. . . .

Vastly Expanding FBI Powers

Section 215 vastly expands the FBI's power to spy on ordinary people living in the United States, including United States citizens and permanent residents. It lets the government obtain personal records or things about *anyone*—from libraries, Internet service providers, hospitals, or any business—merely by asserting that the items are "sought for" an ongoing terrorism investigation. Section 215 threatens individual privacy, because it allows the government free reign to monitor our activities. It also endangers freedom of speech, because the threat of government surveillance inevitably discourages people from speaking out—and especially from disagreeing with the government.

Section 215 amends an obscure law called the Foreign Intelligence Surveillance Act (FISA), which became law in 1978. FISA set out the procedures that the FBI had to follow when it wanted to conduct surveillance for foreign intelligence purposes. The system is extraordinary—not least because the FISA Court meets in secret, almost never publishes its decisions, and allows only the government to appear before it. But of course it applied only to foreign spies. Thanks to the PATRIOT Act, the FBI can now use FISA even in investigations that don't involve foreign spies. In fact, under Section 215 the FBI can now spy on ordinary, law-abiding Americans.

To obtain your personal records or things under Section 215, the FBI does not need to show "probable cause"—or any reason—to believe that you have done anything wrong. It does not need to show that you are involved in terrorism, directly or indirectly, or that you work for a country that sponsors terrorism. If you are a United States citizen or permanent resident, the FBI can obtain a Section 215 order against you based in part on your First Amendment activity—based, for example, on the books that you borrowed from the library, the Web sites you visited, the religious services you attended, or the political organizations that you joined. If you are not a citizen or permanent resident, the FBI can obtain a Section 215 order against you based *solely* on your First Amendment activity.

> **"** *Section 215 authorizes federal officials to fish through personal records and belongings even if they are not investigating any person in particular.* **"**

In fact, Section 215 authorizes federal officials to fish through personal records and belongings even if they are not investigating any person in particular. Under Section 215, the FBI could demand a list of every person who has checked out a particular book on Islamic fundamentalism. It could demand a list of people who had visited a particular Web site. It could demand a client list from a charity that offers social services to immigrants.

A gag order in the law prevents anyone served with a Section 215 order from telling anyone else that the FBI demanded information. Because the gag order remains in effect forever, surveillance targets—even wholly innocent ones—are *never* notified that their privacy has been compromised. If the government uses Section 215 to keep track of the books you read, the Web sites you visit, or the political events you attend, you will simply never know.

The FBI Can Demand Any Records

There is no restriction on the kinds of records or things that the FBI can demand under Section 215. Before the PATRIOT Act, the FBI's authority under this provision was restricted to a discrete category of business records—records from vehicle rental agencies, storage facilities and other similar businesses. Section

215 expands this authority to reach "any tangible things (including books, records, papers, documents, and other items)," held by *any* organization or person. The FBI could use Section 215 to demand:

• personal belongings, such as books, letters, journals, or computers, directly from one's home.

• a list of people who have visited a particular Web site.

• medical records, including psychiatric records.

• a list of people who have borrowed a particular book from a public library.

• a membership list from an advocacy organization like Greenpeace, the Federalist Society, or the ACLU.

• a list of people who worship at a particular church, mosque, temple, or synagogue.

• a list of people who subscribe to a particular periodical.

In fact, the [former] Attorney General [John Ashcroft] himself has acknowledged that the FBI could use the law even more broadly. The following exchange between the Attorney General and Rep. Tammy Baldwin (D-WI) took place before the House Judiciary Committee in June 2003:

> *The FBI can use Section 215 against you even if it knows for a fact that you are not engaged in crime or espionage.*

BALDWIN: Prior to the enactment of the USA PATRIOT Act, a FISA order for business records related only to common carriers, accommodations, storage facilities and vehicle rentals. Is that correct?

ASHCROFT: Yes, it is. . . .

BALDWIN: OK. Now, under section 215 of the USA PATRIOT Act, now the government can obtain any relevant, tangible items. Is that correct?

ASHCROFT: I think they are authorized to ask for relevant, tangible items.

BALDWIN: And so that would include things like book purchase records?

ASHCROFT: . . . [I]n the narrow arena in which they are authorized to ask, yes.

BALDWIN: A library book or computer records?

ASHCROFT: I think it could include a library book or computer records. . . .

BALDWIN: Education records?

ASHCROFT: I think there are some education records that would be susceptible to demand under the court supervision of FISA, yes.

BALDWIN: Genetic information?

ASHCROFT: . . . I think [we] probably could.

Section 215 Violates the Constitution

Section 215 violates the United States Constitution. It violates privacy and due process rights guaranteed by the Fourth Amendment, and free speech rights guaranteed by the First Amendment.

> *The right of the people to be secure in their persons, houses, papers, and effects, against unreasonable searches and seizures, shall not be violated, and no warrants shall issue, but upon probable cause. . . .*
> —United States Constitution, Fourth Amendment

• Section 215 violates the Fourth Amendment by allowing the government to search and seize your personal records or belongings without a warrant and without showing probable cause.

The Fourth Amendment ordinarily prohibits the government from searching your home or office, or from seizing your records, unless it first obtains a warrant based on "probable cause" to believe that you are engaged in criminal activity. The Supreme Court has applied this protection not just to physical objects but to personal records and electronic data. Section 215 does not require the government to obtain a warrant or to establish probable cause before it demands your personal records or belongings. In fact, the FBI can use Section 215 against you even if it knows for a fact that you are not engaged in crime or espionage.

• Section 215 also violates the Fourth Amendment because it does not require the government to provide you with notice—*ever*—that your records or belongings have been seized.

Ordinarily the Constitution requires that the government notify you before it searches or seizes your records or belongings. Indeed, the Supreme Court has held that this "knock and announce" principle is at the core of the Fourth Amendment's protections; without notice, after all, a person whose privacy rights have been violated will never have an opportunity to challenge the government's conduct. While in some circumstances delayed notice is permitted to protect against the destruction of evidence, the Supreme Court has *never* upheld a government search for which notice is never provided.

> *Congress shall make no law . . . abridging the freedom of speech, or of the press; or the right of the people peaceably to assemble, and to petition the government for a redress of grievances.*
> —United States Constitution, First Amendment

• Section 215 violates the First Amendment because it allows the government to easily obtain information about, for example, the books you read, the Web sites you visit, and the religious institutions you attend.

Section 215 expressly authorizes the government to obtain books, records, and other items that are protected by the First Amendment. The FBI could use Section 215 to order a library or bookstore to produce records showing that you had borrowed or bought a particular book. It could force an Internet Service Provider to turn over your email messages or records of which Web sites you've visited. It could demand that a political organization confirm that you participated in a political rally. It could even order a mosque to provide a list of all its members.

The Constitution's warrant and probable cause requirements protect First Amendment interests by prohibiting the government from spying on people based solely on their political views or religious associations. In a 1972 case involving electronic surveillance, the Supreme Court wrote:

> *History abundantly documents the tendency of Government—however benevolent and benign its motives—to view with suspicion those who most fervently dispute its policies. Fourth Amendment protections become the more necessary when the targets of official surveillance may be those suspected of unorthodoxy in their political beliefs.*

Section 215 is likely to chill lawful dissent. If people think that their conversations, their emails, and their reading habits are being monitored, people will feel less comfortable saying what they think—especially if they disagree with government policies. Indeed, there is a real danger that the FBI will wield its

Section 215 power specifically to silence dissenters.

• Section 215 also violates the First Amendment by preventing those served with Section 215 orders from ever telling anyone that the FBI demanded information, even if the information is not tied to a particular suspect and poses no risk to national security.

Section 215 prohibits people who receive orders for personal records or belongings from disclosing that fact to others even where there is no real need for secrecy. The gag order is extremely broad. It prevents people from even telling the press and public that the government has sought records, even if the statement is made in the most general terms, without identifying the specific target of the order. For example, it would prevent a library from publicizing statistics about the number of times the FBI had sought patron records in a given time period. To ensure compliance with the gag order, individual employees served with Section 215 orders must strictly limit telling even their fellow staff members that the FBI has demanded information.

Section 215 gag orders are automatic, and do not require the government to explain to the judge why secrecy is necessary. In other contexts, gag orders are imposed only where the government has made a showing that secrecy is necessary in the particular case. Section 215 gag orders are also indefinite, which means that surveillance targets—even wholly innocent ones—will never know their privacy was compromised. In certain investigations, secrecy may sometimes be necessary, and short-term gag orders may sometimes be unavoidable. But Section 215 gag orders require no necessity and are unlimited. If the First Amendment means anything, it means that the government cannot impose an indefinite gag order without reference to the facts of the particular case.

Targeting Innocent People

Section 215 was *specifically intended* to authorize the FBI to obtain information about innocent people—people who are not engaged in criminal activity or in espionage. Of course, not all innocent people are likely to be equally affected. As it has done in the past, the FBI is once again targeting ethnic, political, and religious minority communities disproportionately. In the war on terrorism, the FBI has unfairly targeted minority and immigrant communities with its surveillance and enforcement efforts. The FBI and the Immigration and Naturalization Service

(INS) rounded up over a thousand immigrants as "special interest" detainees, holding many of them without charges for months. A "Special Registration" program now requires tens of thousands of Arab and Muslim immigrants to submit to a call-in interview from which other immigrants are exempted. During the war in Iraq, many Iraqis and Iraqi-Americans were asked to submit to "voluntary" interviews with the FBI. And a Jan. 28, 2003 *New York Times* article by Eric Lichtblau *("F.B.I. Tells Offices to Count Local Muslims and Mosques")* reported that the FBI ordered its field offices to "establish a yardstick for the number of terrorism investigations and intelligence warrants" by counting the number of Muslims and mosques in their districts.

> *If people think that their conversations, their emails, and their reading habits are being monitored, people will feel less comfortable saying what they think—especially if they disagree with government policies.*

There is little doubt, then, that Section 215 is being used against minorities and immigrants disproportionately. This doesn't make us any safer, of course. (It bears noting, for example, that *none* of the immigrants whom the FBI and INS held as "special interest" detainees was charged with a terrorism-related offense.) Indeed, targeting minorities and immigrants simply because of their ethnicity, religion, or nationality wastes resources that could be dedicated to apprehending real terrorists.

In fact, the FBI does not need the PATRIOT Act to investigate people who are legitimately suspected of engaging in terrorist or criminal activity; it has always had this power. Nor does the FBI need the PATRIOT Act to engage in surveillance of people who are legitimately suspected of spying for foreign governments or terrorist groups; it has had this power since 1978. The government can use these powers—powers that predate the PATRIOT Act—to vigorously pursue terrorists and other criminals, consistent with the Constitution.

14

Fears of Patriot Act Privacy Violations Are Overblown

Heather Mac Donald

Heather Mac Donald is a contributing editor to City Journal *and author of* The Burden of Bad Ideas: How Modern Intellectuals Misshape Our Society. *Her articles have appeared in the* Wall Street Journal, *the* New Republic, *and the* New York Times.

Ever since the USA PATRIOT Act was signed by President George W. Bush in the weeks after the 9/11 terrorist attacks, civil libertarians have been extremely critical of the law because of the expanded investigative powers it gives government agencies. These people seem to forget that America is at war and, under the circumstances, authorities have acted with extreme caution in order to protect privacy rights. The Patriot Act does allow the FBI and CIA to access an individual's personal and financial records, but agents must first appeal to a judge to sign a warrant authorizing the investigation. In addition, many so-called private records are in the hands of third parties, such as banks, libraries, and doctors, and thus are not protected as personal property by the Constitution. Despite the near hysteria generated by critics, the Patriot Act simply updates laws that have been used against organized crime and drug dealers for years. In a post-9/11 world, governments need these expanded powers to protect the citizenry from those who would harm them.

Heather Mac Donald, "Straight Talk on Homeland Security," *City Journal*, Summer 2003. Copyright © 2003 by Manhattan Institute for Policy Research. Reproduced by permission.

The backlash against the Bush administration's War on Terror began on 9/11 and has not let up since. Left- and right-wing advocacy groups have likened the Bush administration to fascists, murderers, apartheid ideologues, and usurpers of basic liberties. Over 120 cities and towns have declared themselves "civil liberties safe zones"; and the press has amplified at top volume a recent report by the Justice Department's inspector general denouncing the government's handling of suspects after 9/11. Even the nation's librarians are shredding documents to safeguard their patrons' privacy and foil government investigations.

The advocates' rhetoric is both false and dangerous. Lost in the blizzard of propaganda is any consciousness that 9/11 was an act of war against the U.S. by foreign enemies concealed within the nation's borders. If the media and political elites keep telling the public that the campaign against those terrorist enemies is just a racist power grab, the most essential weapon against terror cells—intelligence from ordinary civilians—will be jeopardized. A drumbeat of ACLU propaganda could discourage a tip that might be vital in exposing an al-Qaida plot.

> *The enemy . . . is hidden on American soil in the civilian population, with the intention of slaughtering as many innocent noncombatants as possible.*

It is crucial, therefore, to demolish the extravagant lies about the anti-terror initiatives. Close scrutiny of the charges and the reality that they misrepresent shows that civil liberties are fully intact. The majority of legal changes after September 11 simply brought the law into the twenty-first century. In those cases where the government has expanded its powers—as is inevitable during a war—important judicial and statutory safeguards protect the rights of law-abiding citizens. And in the one hard case where a citizen's rights appear to have been curtailed—the detention of a suspected American al-Qaida operative without access to an attorney—that detention is fully justified under the laws of war.

The anti–War on Terror worldview found full expression only hours after the World Trade Center fell, in a remarkable e-mail that spread like wildfire over the Internet that very day.

Sent out by Harvard Law School research fellow John Perry Barlow, founder of the cyber-libertarian Electronic Freedom Foundation, the message read: "Control freaks will dine on this day for the rest of our lives. Within a few hours, we will see beginning the most vigorous efforts to end what remains of freedom in America. . . . I beg you to begin NOW to do whatever you can . . . to prevent the spasm of control mania from destroying the dreams that far more have died for over the last two hundred twenty-five years than died this morning. Don't let the terrorists or (their natural allies) the fascists win. Remember that the goal of terrorism is to create increasingly paralytic totalitarianism in the government it attacks. Don't give them the satisfaction. . . . And, please, let us try to forgive those who have committed these appalling crimes. If we hate them, we will become them."

Barlow, a former lyricist for the Grateful Dead, epitomizes the rise of the sixties counterculture into today's opinion elite, for whom no foreign enemy could ever pose as great a threat to freedom as the U.S. For Barlow, the problem isn't the obvious evil of Islamic terrorism but the imputed evil of the American government—an inversion that would characterize the next two years of anti-administration jeremiads. In this spirit, critics would measure each legal change not against the threat it responded to, but in a vacuum. Their verdict: "increasingly paralytic totalitarianism."

Right-wing libertarians soon joined forces with the Left. A few months after the Twin Towers fell, the Rutherford Institute, a Christian think tank concerned with religious liberty, added the final piece to the anti-administration argument: the 9/11 attacks were not war but, at most, a crime. Rutherford president John Whitehead denounced the Bush administration's characterization of the terror strikes as "acts of war by foreign aggressors," without however offering a single argument to support his view. Since that characterization has produced, in Whitehead's view, growing "police statism" that is destroying Americans' freedom, the characterization must be false.

An Act of War

In fact, of course, the 9/11 bombings were classic decapitation strikes, designed to take out America's political and financial leadership. Had a state carried them out, no one could possibly deny that they were acts of war. . . . The aim of the 19 foreign terrorists and their backers was not criminal but ideological: to revenge U.S. policies in the Middle East with mass destruction.

Recognizing that the World Trade Center and Pentagon attacks were acts of war entails certain consequences. First, the campaign against al-Qaida and other Islamic terror organizations is really war, not a metaphor, like the "war on drugs." Second, it is a war unlike any the U.S. has ever fought. The enemy, mostly but not exclusively foreign, is hidden on American soil in the civilian population, with the intention of slaughtering as many innocent noncombatants as possible. The use of military force abroad, while necessary, is by no means sufficient: domestic counterterrorism efforts by the FBI and other domestic law enforcement agencies are at least as essential to defeating the enemy.

When these agencies are operating against Islamic terrorists, they are operating in an unprecedented war mode—but most of the rules that govern them were designed for crime fighting. The tension between the Justice Department's and FBI's traditional roles as law enforcement agencies and their new roles as terror warriors lies at the heart of the battle over the Bush administration's post-9/11 homeland-security policies: critics refuse to recognize the reality of the war and thus won't accept the need for expanded powers to prosecute it.

> *// From the moment the administration proposed the legislation, defenders of the status quo started ringing the tyranny alarm. //*

Most of the changes in the law that the Justice Department sought after 9/11 concern the department's ability to gather intelligence on terror strikes before they happen—its key responsibility in the terror war. Yet the libertarian lobby will not allow the department to budge from the crime paradigm, refusing to admit that surveillance and evidence-gathering rules designed to protect the rights of suspected car thieves and bank robbers may need modification when the goal is preventing a suitcase bomb from taking out JFK [International Airport]. But of course the libertarians rarely acknowledge that suitcase bombs and the like are central to this debate.

Ironically, none of the changes instituted by [former] Attorney General [John] Ashcroft comes anywhere near what the government *could* ask for in wartime, such as the suspension of *habeas corpus* [the right of a detainee to plead his case before a judge], as Lincoln ordered during the Civil War. The changes preserve intact the entire criminal procedural framework governing normal FBI and police actions, and merely tinker around the edges. But the left and right civil libertarians are having none of it.

Patriot Act Hysteria

The charges they have brought against the War on Terror have been so numerous, impugning every single administration action since 9/11, that it would take hundreds of pages to refute them all. But the following analysis of only the main charges will amply illustrate the range of duplicitous strategies that the anti-government forces deploy.

Strategy #1: Hide the Judge Jan O'Rourke, a librarian in Bucks County, Pennsylvania, is preparing for the inevitable post-9/11 assault: She is destroying all records of her patrons' book and Internet use and is advising other Bucks County libraries to do the same. The object of her fear? The U.S. government. O'Rourke is convinced that federal spooks will soon knock on her door to spy on her law-abiding clients' reading habits. So, like thousands of librarians across the country, she is making sure that when that knock comes, she will have nothing to show. "If we don't have the information, then they can't get it," she explains.

O'Rourke is suffering from Patriot Act hysteria, a malady approaching epidemic levels. The USA-PATRIOT Act, which President Bush signed in October 2001, is a complex measure to boost the federal government's ability to detect and prevent terrorism. Its most important provision relaxed a judge-made rule that, especially after Clinton administration strengthening, had prevented intelligence and law enforcement officials from sharing information and collaborating on terror investigations. But the act made many other needed changes too: updating surveillance law to take into account new communications technology, for instance, enhancing the Treasury Department's ability to disrupt terrorist financing networks, and modestly increasing the attorney general's power to detain and deport suspected terrorist aliens.

From the moment the administration proposed the legislation, defenders of the status quo started ringing the tyranny alarm. When the law passed, the Electronic Privacy Information Center depicted a tombstone on its website, captioned: "The Fourth Amendment: 1789–2001." The *Washington Post* denounced the bill as "panicky." And the evertouchy American Library Association decided that a particular provision of the Patriot Act—section 215—was a "present danger to the constitutional rights and privacy of library users," though the section says not a word about libraries.

The furor over section 215 is a case study in Patriot Act fearmongering. Section 215 allows the FBI to seek business records in the hands of third parties—the enrollment application of a Saudi national in an American flight school, say—while investigating terrorism. The section broadens the categories of institutions whose records and other "tangible items" the government may seek in espionage and terror cases, on the post-9/11 recognition that lawmakers cannot anticipate what sorts of organizations terrorists may exploit. In the past, it may have been enough to get hotel bills or storage-locker contracts (two of the four categories of records covered in the narrower law that section 215 replaced) to trace the steps of a Soviet spy; today, however, gumshoes may find they need receipts from scuba-diving schools or farm-supply stores to piece together a plot to blow up the Golden Gate Bridge. Section 215 removed the requirement that the records must concern an "agent of a foreign power" (generally, a spy or terrorist), since, again, the scope of an anti-terror investigation is hard to predict in advance.

> *The battleground is not the courtroom but the world beyond, where speed and secrecy can mean life or death.*

From this tiny acorn, Bush administration foes have conjured forth a mighty assault on the First Amendment. The ACLU warns that with section 215, "the FBI could spy on a person because they don't like the books she reads, or because they don't like the websites she visits. They could spy on her because she wrote a letter to the editor that criticized government policy." Stanford Law School dean Kathleen Sullivan calls section 215 "threatening." And librarians, certain that the section is all about them, are scaring library users with signs warning that the government may spy on their reading habits.

These charges are nonsense. Critics of section 215 deliberately ignore the fact that any request for items under the section requires judicial approval. An FBI agent cannot simply walk into a flight school or library and demand records. The bureau must first convince the court that oversees anti-terror investigations (the Foreign Intelligence Surveillance Act, or FISA, court) that the documents are relevant to protecting "against international terrorism or clandestine intelligence activities." The chance that the FISA court will approve a 215 order because the FBI "doesn't like the books [a person] reads . . . or because she wrote a letter to the editor that criticized government policy" is zero. If the bureau can show that someone using the Bucks County library computers to surf the web and send e-mails has traveled to Pakistan and was seen with other terror suspects in Virginia, on the other hand, then the court may well grant an order to get the library's Internet logs.

Moreover, before the FBI can even approach the FISA court with any kind of request, agents must have gone through multiple levels of bureaucratic review just to open an anti-terror investigation. And to investigate a U.S. citizen (rather than an alien) under FISA, the FBI must show that he is knowingly engaged in terrorism or espionage.

Ignoring the Patriot Act's strict judicial review requirements is the most common strategy of the act's critics. Time and again, the [critics] will hold up a section from the bill as an example of rampaging executive power—without ever mentioning that the power in question is overseen by federal judges who will allow its use only if the FBI can prove its relevance to a bona fide terror (or sometimes criminal) investigation. By contrast, in the few cases where a law enforcement power does not require judicial review, the jackboots-are-coming brigade screams for judges as the only trustworthy check on executive tyranny.

No Right to Privacy

Strategy #2: Invent New Rights A running theme of the campaign against section 215 and many other Patriot Act provisions is that they violate the Fourth Amendment right to privacy. But there is no Fourth Amendment privacy right in records or other items disclosed to third parties. A credit-card user, for example, reveals his purchases to the seller and to the credit-card company. He therefore has no privacy expectations in the record of those purchases that the Fourth Amendment would protect. As a result, the government, whether in a criminal case or a terror investigation, may seek his credit-card receipts without a traditional Fourth Amendment showing to a court that there is "probable cause" to believe that a crime has been or is about to be committed. Instead, terror investigators must convince the FISA court that the receipts are "relevant."

Despite librarians' fervent belief to the contrary, this analysis applies equally to library patrons' book borrowing or Internet use. The government may obtain those records without violating anyone's Fourth Amendment rights, because the patron has already revealed his borrowing and web browsing to library staff, other readers (in the days of handwritten book checkout cards), and Internet service providers. Tombstones declaring the death of the Fourth Amendment contain no truth whatsoever.

What's different in the section 215 provisions is that libraries or other organizations can't challenge the FISA court's order and can't inform the target of the investigation, as they can in ordinary criminal proceedings. But that difference is crucial for the Justice Department's war-making function. The department wants to know if an al-Qaida suspect has consulted maps of the Croton reservoir and researched the toxic capacities of cyanide in the New York Public Library not in order to win a conviction for poisoning New York's water supply but to preempt the plot before it happens. The battleground is not the courtroom but the world beyond, where speed and secrecy can mean life or death.

Strategy #3: Demand Antiquated Laws The librarians' crusade against section 215 has drawn wide media attention and triggered an ongoing congressional battle, led by Vermont socialist Bernie Sanders, to pass a law purporting to protect the "Freedom to Read." But the publicity that administration-hostile librarians were able to stir up pales in comparison to the clout of the Internet privacy lobby. The day the Patriot Act became law, the Center for Democracy and Technology sent around a warning that "privacy standards" had been "gutt[ed]." The Electronic Freedom Foundation declared that the "civil liberties of ordinary Americans have taken a tremendous blow." Jeffrey Rosen of *The New Republic* claimed that the law gave the government "essentially unlimited authority" to surveil Americans. The ACLU asserted that the FBI had suddenly gained "wide powers of phone and internet surveillance." And the *Washington Post* editorialized that the act made it "easier" to wiretap by "lowering the standard of judicial review."

The target of this ire? A section that merely updates existing law to modern technology. The government has long had the power to collect the numbers dialed from, or the incoming numbers to, a person's telephone by showing a court that the information is "relevant to an ongoing criminal investigation." Just as in section 215 of the Patriot Act, this legal standard is lower than traditional Fourth Amendment "probable cause," because the phone user has already forfeited any constitutional privacy rights he may have in his phone number or the number he calls by revealing them to the phone company.

> *The government may expand its powers to detect terrorism without diminishing civil liberties one iota, as long as those powers remain subject to traditional restraints.*

A 1986 federal law tried to extend the procedures for collecting phone-number information to electronic communications, but it was so poorly drafted that its application to e-mail remained unclear. Section 216 of the Patriot Act resolves the ambiguity by making clear that the rules for obtaining phone numbers apply to incoming and outgoing e-mail addresses as well. The government can obtain e-mail headers—but not content—by showing a court that the information is "relevant to an ongoing criminal investigation." Contrary to cyber-libertarian howls, this is not a vast new power to spy but merely the logical extension of an existing power to a new form of communication. Nothing else has changed: the standard for obtaining information about the source or destination of a communication is the same as always.

Section 216 made one other change to communications surveillance law. When a court issues an order allowing the collection of phone numbers or e-mail headers, that order now applies nationally. Before, if a phone call was transmitted by a chain of phone companies headquartered in different states, investigators needed approval from a court in each of those states to track it. This time-consuming procedure could not be more dangerous in the age of terror. As Attorney General John Ashcroft testified in September 2001, the "ability of law enforcement officers to trace communications into different jurisdictions without obtaining an additional court order can be the difference between life and death for American citizens." Yet the ACLU has complained that issuing national warrants for phone and e-mail routing information marginalizes the judiciary and gives law enforcement unchecked power to search citizens.

The furor over this section of the Patriot Act employs the same deceptions as the furor over section 215 (the business records provision). In both cases, Patriot Act bashers ignore the fact that a court must approve the government's access to information. Despite the *Washington Post*'s assertion to the contrary, section 216 does not lower any standards of judicial review. Both the anti-216 and anti-215 campaigns fabricate privacy rights where none exists. And neither of these anti-government campaigns lets one iota of the reality of terrorism intrude into its analyses of fictional rights violations—the reality that communications technology is essential to an enemy that has no geographical locus, and whose combatants have mastered the Internet and every form of modern communications, along with methods to defeat surveillance, such as using and discarding multiple cell phones and communicating from Internet cafés. The anti–Patriot Act forces would keep anti-terror law enforcement in the world of [the old telephone company known as] Ma Bell and rotary phones, even as America's would-be destroyers use America's most sophisticated technology against it. . . .

When the War on Terror's opponents intone, "We need not trade liberty for security," they are right—but not in the way they think. Contrary to their slogan's assumption, there is no zero-sum relationship between liberty and security. The government may expand its powers to detect terrorism without diminishing civil liberties one iota, as long as those powers remain subject to traditional restraints: statutory prerequisites for investigative action, judicial review, and political accountability. So far, these conditions have been met.

But the larger fallacy at the heart of the elites' liberty-versus-security formula is its blindness to all threats to freedom that do not emanate from the White House. Nothing the Bush administration has done comes close to causing the loss of freedom that Americans experienced after 9/11, when air travel shut down for days, and fear kept hundreds of thousands shut up in their homes. Should al-Qaida strike again, fear will once again paralyze the country far beyond the effects of any possible government restriction on civil rights. And that is what the government is trying to forestall, in the knowledge that preserving security is essential to preserving freedom.

15

Widespread Use of Social Security Numbers Abets Identity Theft

Sheila R. Cherry

Sheila R. Cherry is a journalist who writes extensively about government affairs for Insight on the News, *a national biweekly newsmagazine published in Washington, D.C., by the Washington Times Corporation.*

When the Social Security number was created in 1936, it was intended to be used solely as an identifier for workers earning benefits. Since that time, it has become a national identification number used by banks, governments, employers, and a host of other entities. This expanded use of the Social Security number has provided criminals with an easy method for stealing identity. With a stolen Social Security number, identity thieves can cause financial ruin for victims by fraudulently obtaining credit cards, bank and car loans, and other financial benefits. Until the government restricts the use of Social Security numbers, the number of people suffering from identity theft will only continue to rise.

Identity theft is on the rise, said Howard Beales, director of the Bureau of Consumer Protection for the Federal Trade Commission (FTC), in testimony before the Senate Judiciary Committee in March [2002]. For calendar year 2001, the FTC's Identity Theft Data Clearinghouse database received more than 86,000 complaints from victims of ID theft, Beales told the

Shelia R. Cherry, "Keep an Eye on Who Gets Your Number: The Social Security Number Has Become the National Identification Code—One Fraught with Security Loopholes and Serious Implications for Privacy Rights," *Insight on the News,* July 15, 2002. Copyright © 2002 by News World Communications, Inc. All rights reserved. Reproduced with permission.

panel. According to the General Accounting Office (GAO), SSNs [Social Security numbers] often are the "identifier" of choice among identity thieves.

Yet even as the FTC and consumer advocates seek to strengthen privacy protections, say security specialists, it appears that federal, state and local governments may be the weakest link in improper SSN disclosures. "In the course of using SSNs to administer their programs, and as employers, agencies sometimes display these SSNs on documents, such as program-eligibility cards or employee badges, that can be seen by others who may have no need for the SSN," the GAO reported in May [2002].

> **❝ The SSN is the key to your credit and banking accounts and is the prime target of criminals. ❞**

The SSN has become one of the clearest examples of government "mission creep." When created in 1936, the SSN was presented as a unique identifier whose sole purpose would be to track the earnings of workers eligible to receive Social Security benefits. But, as explained by the GAO, on Nov. 25, 1943, President Franklin D. Roosevelt issued Executive Order 9397 expanding the use of the SSN for all federal agencies "to use identification systems for individuals, rather than set up a new identification system."

Balancing Needs and Rights

The Privacy Rights Clearinghouse (PRC), a San Diego–based nonprofit [corporation] that teaches consumers how to protect their personal privacy, advises citizens to release their SSNs only when absolutely necessary—as is required on tax forms, employment records and banking, stock and property transactions. "The SSN is the key to your credit and banking accounts and is the prime target of criminals," the PRC warns.

The PRC's Website advises: "If a business requests your SSN, ask if it has an alternative number which can be used instead. Speak to a manager or supervisor if your request is not heeded. Ask to see the company's policy on SSNs. If necessary, take your business elsewhere."

That is widely regarded as sagacity in the private sector. But similar care during a government interaction is likely to provoke a cold stare and a chilly reaction. "If the SSN is requested by a government agency, look for the Privacy Act notice," the site continues. "This will tell you if your SSN is required, what will be done with it and what happens if you refuse to provide it."

The purpose of the Privacy Act, the GAO reported in May, is to balance the government's need to maintain information about individuals with the rights of individuals to be protected against unwarranted invasions of their privacy by federal agencies. Under the act, individuals can bring a civil action against a federal agency requesting the SSN if they believe that the agency has not complied with the Section 7 requirements and if this failure to comply results in an adverse effect on the individual.

> *While the victim and his wife spent more than four years and more than $15,000 of their own money to restore their credit and reputation, the criminal served a brief sentence.*

Nevertheless, the GAO auditors found that although nearly all government entities surveyed collect and use SSNs for a variety of reasons, many reported they do not consistently provide individuals with information required by the Privacy Act. Furthermore, the GAO officials found, "Although agencies that use SSNs to provide benefits and services are taking steps to safeguard the numbers from improper disclosure, our survey identified potential weaknesses in the security of information systems at all levels of government." The weaknesses discovered indicate that SSNs may be at risk of improper disclosure by bureaucrats who see their primary responsibility as preserving the integrity of their records and data rather than protecting the privacy of the people to whom the data relate.

For example, the Department of Criminal Justice in a state with a workforce of 40,000 employees displays SSNs on all of its employee-identification cards. The GAO auditors reported that employees had to tape over these numbers on their badges so that prison inmates and others could not view their personal information.

Rep. E. Clay Shaw (R-Fla.), chairman of the House Ways and

116

Means subcommittee on Social Security, responded to the report by indicating that the problem has the potential to worsen. "Most alarming is that government agencies are increasingly putting SSNs on the Internet. We cannot allow this to happen," he said in a written statement. . . .

A Credit Nightmare

Meanwhile average citizens, such as those state criminal-justice workers discussed above, are on their own about how best to shield their private information from brazen offenses such as one a Department of Justice (DOJ) Webpage dubbed a "notorious case of identity theft." A convicted felon, the DOJ says, "not only incurred more than $100,000 of credit-card debt, obtained a federal home loan and bought homes, motorcycles and handguns in the victim's name, but called his victim to taunt him—saying that he could continue to pose as the victim for as long as he wanted because identity theft was not a federal crime at that time—before filing for bankruptcy, also in the victim's name."

> **"**ID thieves can take over your accounts, open new ones in your name, get utility service, apply for government benefits, file for bankruptcy, even get married in your name. **"**

Adding to the insult, according to the DOJ, "While the victim and his wife spent more than four years and more than $15,000 of their own money to restore their credit and reputation, the criminal served a brief sentence for making a false statement to procure a firearm, but made no restitution to his victim for any of the harm he had caused. This case, and others like it, prompted Congress in 1998 to create a new federal offense of identity theft."

Now the National Consumers League (NCL), a membership-based consumer organization, has teamed with the Bank of America to launch a new campaign to help educate consumers about identity theft. And individuals aren't the only ones to suffer from such fraud. In a rare private-sector admission, the Bank of America candidly acknowledged that it had fallen victim to ID fraud earlier this year [2002] when consumers received an e-mail from someone pretending to be from the bank. The e-mail directed Bank of America customers to a Website masquerading as Bank of America's. Once there, the unsuspecting customers were instructed to provide their personal financial information until Bank of America learned about the scam and alerted law-enforcement authorities, who shut down the fraudulent Website.

According to the NCL, its new "Invasion of the ID Snatchers" Webpages (www.nclnet.org) will present common scenarios to illustrate how thieves steal personal information and what they can do with it, tips for consumers on how to avoid ID theft and information about how to report the crime. It also will provide tips for businesses on how to secure the personal information they collect from consumers.

In a written statement, Susan Grant, NCL's vice president for public policy, echoed the DOJ's recognition of a scary new reality. "Depending on the information they steal, ID thieves can take over your accounts, open new ones in your name, get utility service, apply for government benefits, file for bankruptcy, even get married in your name," she said.

Private-sector vigilance may have to set the example for cash-strapped state and local governments that seem increasingly to view the private information of citizens as a state-owned commodity. An example is badly needed. "When comparing the sharing practices of courts, state licensing agencies and county recorders to program agencies that collect and use SSNs, a higher percentage of county recorders reported sharing information containing SSNs with credit bureaus, researchers, debt-collection agencies, private investigators and marketing companies," the GAO reported. Moreover, it added, the local governments that share data often do not restrict receiver use or disclosure of the data.

Sen. Charles Grassley (R-Iowa), ranking member of the Senate Judiciary subcommittee on Crime and Drugs, has joined with Sens. Dianne Feinstein (D-Calif.), Jon Kyl (R-Ariz.) and Jeff Sessions (R-Ala.) in introducing legislation to increase penalties for individuals who commit crimes while using a stolen identity. Grassley puts the onus for SSN vulnerability on the entity that started it. "As the creator of Social Security numbers, the federal government also has to be the protector of Social Security numbers," he says.

Organizations to Contact

The editors have compiled the following list of organizations concerned with the issues debated in this book. The descriptions are derived from materials provided by the organizations. All have publications or information available for interested readers. The list was compiled on the date of publication of the present volume; the information provided here may change. Be aware that many organizations take several weeks or longer to respond to inquiries, so allow as much time as possible.

American Civil Liberties Union (ACLU)
125 Broad St., 18th Fl., New York, NY 10004-2400
(212) 549-2500
e-mail: aclu@aclu.org • Web site: www.aclu.org

The ACLU is a national organization that works to defend civil rights guaranteed in the Constitution. It publishes various materials on civil liberties, including the newsletter *Civil Liberties* and a set of handbooks on individual rights.

Central Intelligence Agency (CIA)
Office of Public Affairs, Washington, DC 20505
(703) 482-0623 • fax: (703) 482-1739
Web site: www.cia.gov

The CIA was created in 1947 with the signing of the National Security Act (NSA) by then-president Harry S. Truman. The NSA charged the director of central intelligence (DCI) with coordinating the nation's intelligence activities and correlating, evaluating, and disseminating intelligence that affects national security. The CIA is an independent agency, responsible to the president through the DCI and accountable to the American people through the Intelligence Oversight Committee of the U.S. Congress. Publications, including *Factbook on Intelligence* and *Report of Investigation—Volume II: The Contra Story*, are available on its Web site.

Electronic Frontier Foundation (EFF)
PO Box 170190, San Francisco, CA 94117
(415) 668-7171 • fax: (415) 668-7007
e-mail: eff@eff.org • Web site: www.eff.org

EFF is an organization that aims to promote a better understanding of telecommunications issues. It fosters awareness of civil liberties issues arising from advancements in computer-based communications media and supports litigation to preserve, protect, and extend First Amendment rights in computing and telecommunications technologies. EFF's publications include *Building the Open Road, Crime and Puzzlement*, the quarterly newsletter *Networks & Policy*, the biweekly electronic newsletter *EFFector Online*, and online bulletins and publications, including *First Amendment in Cyberspace*.

Electronic Privacy Information Center (EPIC)
1718 Connecticut Ave. NW, Suite 200, Washington, DC 20009
(202) 483-1140 • fax: (202) 483-1248
e-mail: info@epic.org • Web site: www.epic.org

EPIC is an organization that advocates the public's right to electronic privacy. It sponsors educational and research programs, compiles statistics, and conducts litigation. Its publications include the biweekly electronic newsletter *EPIC Alert* and online reports.

Federal Bureau of Investigation (FBI)
935 Pennsylvania Ave. NW, Rm. 7972, Washington, DC 20535
(202) 324-3000
Web site: www.fbi.gov

The FBI, the principal investigative arm of the U.S. Department of Justice, has the authority and responsibility to investigate specific crimes assigned to it. The FBI also is authorized to provide other law enforcement agencies with cooperative services such as fingerprint identification, laboratory examinations, and police training. The mission of the FBI is to uphold the law through the investigation of violations of federal criminal law; to protect the United States from foreign intelligence and terrorist activities; to provide leadership and law enforcement assistance to federal, state, local, and international agencies; and to perform these responsibilities in a manner that is responsive to the needs of the public and is faithful to the Constitution of the United States. Press releases, congressional statements, and major speeches on issues concerning the FBI are available on the agency's Web site.

Federal Trade Commission (FTC)
600 Pennsylvania Ave. NW, Washington, DC 20580
(877) FTC-HELP (382-4357)
Web site: www.consumer.gov/idtheft/index.html

The Federal Trade Commission works to ensure that the nation's markets are vigorous, efficient, and free of restrictions that harm consumers. The FTC enforces federal consumer-protection laws that prevent fraud, deception, and unfair business practices and combats identity theft, Internet scams, and telemarketing fraud. Publications are available on the FTC Web site with consumer information concerning telemarketing, credit cards, and identity theft.

First Amendment Center at Vanderbilt University
1207 Eighteenth Ave. South, Nashville, TN 37212
(615) 727-1600 • fax: (615) 727-1319
e-mail: info@fac.org • Web site: www.firstamendmentcenter.org

The First Amendment Center works to preserve and protect First Amendment freedoms through information and education. The center serves as a forum for the study and exploration of free expression issues, including freedom of speech, of the press, of religion, and the right to assemble and petition the government. The center publishes the annual *State of the First Amendment Report* and has dozens of publications concerning free speech, freedom of the press, and religious liberty available on its Web site.

Health Privacy Project
1120 Nineteenth St. NW, 8th Fl., Washington, DC 20036
(202) 721-5632 • fax: (202) 530-0128
e-mail: info@healthprivacy.org • Web site: www.healthprivacy.org

The Health Privacy Project is dedicated to raising public awareness of the importance of ensuring health privacy in order to improve health care access and quality, both on an individual and a community level. Founded in 1997, the Health Privacy Project provides research studies, policy analyses, congressional testimony, extensive work with the media, and a Web site with information for those concerned with health care issues. The project publishes fact sheets, editorials, press releases, privacy regulations guides, and reports on health privacy.

Heritage Foundation
214 Massachusetts Ave. NE, Washington, DC 20002
(202) 546-4400 • (800) 544-4843 • fax: (202) 544-2260
e-mail: pubs@heritage.org • Web site: www.heritage.org

The Heritage Foundation is a conservative public policy research institute that supports the principles of free enterprise and limited government. Its many publications include the monthly *Policy Review* and position papers concerning terrorism, privacy rights, and constitutional issues.

Hoover Institution
Stanford University, Stanford, CA 94305-6010
(650) 723-1754 • (877) 466-8374
Web site: www-hoover.stanford.edu

The Hoover Institution on War, Revolution and Peace at Stanford University is a conservative public policy research center devoted to advanced study of politics, economics, and political economy—both domestic and foreign—as well as international affairs. The institution hosts world-renowned scholars and ongoing programs of policy-oriented research. Its many publications include *Weekly Essays, Hoover Digest, Education Next,* and *Policy Review.*

Manhattan Institute
52 Vanderbilt Ave., New York, NY 10017
(212) 599-7000 • fax: (212) 599-3494
e-mail: lyoung@manhattan-institute.org
Web site: www.manhattan-institute.org

The Manhattan Institute is a conservative think tank that supports and publicizes research on challenging urban-policy issues such as taxes, welfare, crime, the legal system, city life, race, education, and other topics. The institute publishes a wide variety of books, articles, opinion pieces, reports, and speeches and the quarterly magazine *City Journal.*

National Security Agency (NSA)
9800 Savage Rd., Ft. Meade, MD 20755-6248
(301) 688-6524
Web site: www.nsa.gov

The National Security Agency coordinates, directs, and performs activities such as designing cipher systems, which protect American information systems and produce foreign intelligence information. The NSA employs satellites to collect data from telephones and computers, aiding in the fight against terrorism. Speeches, briefings, and reports are available on its Web site.

National Workrights Institute
166 Wall St., Princeton, NJ 08540
(609) 683 0313
e-mail: info@workrights.org • Web site: www.workrights.org

The National Workrights Institute was founded in January 2000 by the former staff of the American Civil Liberties Union's National Taskforce on Civil Liberties in the Workplace. The institute's goal is to improve the legal protection of human rights in the workplace and to see that employment laws are adequately enforced and strengthened. The institute publishes annual reports and provides information for articles in newspapers, national magazines, and television shows, including the *New York Times, Washington Post, Los Angeles Times, Christian Science Monitor, U.S. News & World Report, Crossfire*, NPR, and *ABC World News Tonight.*

Privacy International
1718 Connecticut Ave. NW, Suite 200, Washington, DC 20009
(202) 483-1217 • fax: (202) 483-1248
e-mail: privacyint@privacy.org • Web site: www.privacy.org

Privacy International is an independent, nongovernment organization whose goal is to protect the privacy rights—threatened by increasing technology—of citizens worldwide. On its Web site the organization provides archives of material on privacy, including international agreements, the report *Freedom of Information and Access to Government Records Around the World*, and *Private Parts Online*, an online newsletter that reports recent stories on international privacy issues.

Privacy Rights Clearinghouse (PRC)
3100 Fifth Ave., Suite B, San Diego, CA 92103
(619) 298-3396 • fax: (619) 298-5681
e-mail: jbeebe@privacyrights.org • Web site: www.privacyrights.org

The Privacy Rights Clearinghouse is a nonprofit consumer organization with a two-part mission—to provide consumer information and to advocate for consumer privacy. The PRC's goals are to raise consumer awareness of how technology affects personal privacy; empower consumers to take action to control their own personal information by providing practical tips on privacy protection; respond to specific privacy-related complaints from consumers; and report the nature of consumers' complaints in policy papers, testimony, and speeches. PRC's Web site provides texts of all fact sheets, transcripts of PRC speeches and testimony, FAQs, and stories of consumer experiences.

Bibliography

Books

George J. Annas
The Rights of Patients: The Authoritative ACLU Guide to the Rights of Patients. Carbondale: Southern Illinois University Press, 2004.

David Brin
The Transparent Society: Will Technology Force Us to Choose Between Privacy and Freedom? Reading, MA: Addison Wesley, 1998.

Clay Calvert
Voyeur Nation: Media, Privacy, and Peering in Modern Culture. Boulder, CO: Westview, 2000.

Nancy Change
Silencing Political Dissent. New York: Seven Stories, 2002.

Jamie Court
Corporateering: How Corporate Power Steals Your Personal Freedom—and What You Can Do About It. New York: Jeremy P. Tarcher/Putnam, 2003.

James X. Dempsey and David Cole
Terrorism and the Constitution: Sacrificing Civil Liberties in the Name of National Security. Washington, DC: First Amendment Foundation, 2002.

Joseph W. Eaton
The Privacy Card: A Low Cost Strategy to Combat Terrorism. Lanham, MD: Rowman & Littlefield, 2003.

Herbert N. Foerstel
Refuge of a Scoundrel: The Patriot Act in Libraries. Westport, CT: Libraries Unlimited, 2004.

Simson Garfinkel
Database Nation: The Death of Privacy in the 21st Century. Cambridge, MA: O'Reilly, 2000.

Eric J. Gertler
Prying Eyes: Protect Your Privacy from People Who Sell to You, Snoop on You, and Steal from You. New York: Random House Reference, 2004.

John Hagel III and Marc Singer
Net Worth: Shaping Markets When Customers Make the Rules. Boston: Harvard Business School Press, 1999.

Richard Hunter
World Without Secrets: Business, Crime, and Privacy in the Age of Ubiquitous Computing. New York: John Wiley, 2002.

Bruce Kasanoff
Making It Personal: How to Profit from Personalization Without Invading Privacy. Cambridge, MA: Perseus, 2001.

Frederick S. Lane
The Naked Employee: How Technology Is Compromising Workplace Privacy. New York: AMACOM, American Management Association, 2003.

David Lyon	*Surveillance After September 11*. Cambridge, UK: Polity Press, 2003.
Raneta Lawson Mack and Michael J. Kelly	*Equal Justice in the Balance: America's Legal Responses to the Emerging Terrorist Threat*. Ann Arbor: University of Michigan Press, 2004.
C. William Michaels	*No Greater Threat: America After September 11 and the Rise of a National Security State*. New York: Algora, 2002.
Mark Monmonier	*Spying with Maps: Surveillance Technologies and the Future of Privacy*. Chicago: University of Chicago Press, 2002.
Donald J. Musch, ed.	*Civil Liberties and the Foreign Intelligence Surveillance Act*. Dobbs Ferry, NY: Oceana, 2003.
U.S. Congress	*Tools Against Terror: How the Administration Is Implementing New Laws in the Fight to Protect Our Homeland*. Washington, DC: U.S. Government Printing Office, 2004.
Reg Whitaker	*The End of Privacy: How Total Surveillance Is Becoming a Reality*. New York: New Press, 1999.

Periodicals

Sheri A. Alpert	"Protecting Medical Privacy: Challenges in the Age of Genetic Information," *Journal of Social Issues*, Summer 2003.
Stephen Barlas	"Physicians Groups Decry Bush Privacy Proposals," *Psychiatric Times*, June 1, 2002.
Phil E. Benjamin	"The Nation's Health Workers' Safety: Bush Scuttles Medical Privacy," *People's Weekly World*, August 17, 2002.
Eric Chabrow	"E-Government: Benefits Versus Privacy," *Information Week*, April 14, 2003.
Lee Chisun	"Red Means Big Brother's in Charge," *Village Voice*, April 23–29, 2003.
Adam Clymer	"Big Brother vs. Terrorist in Spy Camera Debate," *New York Times*, June 19, 2002.
Patricia Daukantas	"Agencies Must Reach Out to Citizens on Their Data Privacy Concerns, Experts Say," *Government Computer News*, April 7, 2003.
Michael Freeny	"No Hiding Place: Will Patient Privacy Become a Thing of the Past?" *Psychotherapy Networker*, March/April 2003.
Mary P. Gallagher	"FBI Is Upheld in Use of Device That Monitors Keystrokes on Computer: Government Doesn't Have to Explain Technology's Specifics," *New Jersey Law Journal*, December 31, 2001.
Andrew Goldstein	"Mr. Quarantine, Meet Miss Liberty," *Time*, April 8, 2002.

Paul Hill — "Patriot Act Nixes Privacy," *People's Weekly World*, August 21, 2004.

Henry E. Hockeimer Jr. — "USA Patriot Act Is Broader than You Might Imagine; from Libraries to Universities to Trucking Companies, Sweeping Provisions of the Act Change the Status Quo," *New Jersey Law Journal*, April 15, 2002.

Mike Holderness — "Every Step You Take: Making Government Databases Fit the Best Standards of Compatibility Is What Will Destroy Privacy, Not Surveillance," *New Scientist*, May 25, 2002.

Sharon Lerner — "A Reason to Fear," *Village Voice*, March 10–16, 2004.

Steven Levy — "Can Snooping Stop Terrorism? A Data-Mining Initiative Requires Openness and Unimpeachable Leadership. The Department of Defense's TIA Flunked on Both Counts," *Newsweek*, October 13, 2003.

Eric Lichtblau — "Administration Sets Forth a Limited View on Privacy," *New York Times*, March 6, 2002.

Gary T. Marx — "A Tack in the Shoe: Neutralizing and Resisting the New Surveillance," *Journal of Social Issues*, Summer 2003.

Sharlene A. McEvoy — "E-mail and Internet Monitoring and the Workplace: Do Employees Have a Right to Privacy?" *Communications and the Law*, June 2002.

Gene Mirabelli — "O BIG BROTHER, WHERE ART THOU? A Special Report on Homeland Security and a Return to the Dark Ages of Political Surveillance, Citizen Harassment and Government Secrecy," *Metroland*, December 5, 2002.

Lisa Napoli — "Frequent Search Engine Users, Google Is Watching and Counting," *New York Times*, October 6, 2003.

Nina Riccio — "To Test or Not to Test? Random Drug Testing: Is It a Valuable Tool or a Personal Violation?" *Current Health 2*, March 2003.

Bernd Carsten Stahl — "Responsibility for Information Assurance and Privacy: A Problem of Individual Ethics?" *Journal of Organizational and End User Computing*, July–September 2004.

Chris Taylor — "What Spies Beneath: Have You Checked Your PC for Spyware Lately? National Security Could Be at Stake. Your Privacy Too," *Time*, October 7, 2002.

Alan F. Westin — "Social and Political Dimensions of Privacy," *Journal of Social Issues*, Summer 2003.

Index

125

WITHDRAWN

AUG 1 2 2022

By: Jm